PRESIDENTIAL TRIVIA

PRESIDENTIAL TRIVIA

COMPILED BY ERNIE COUCH

Rutledge Hill Press
Nashville, Tennessee

Published in Nashville, Tennessee, by Rutledge Hill Press, Inc.
211 Seventh Avenue North, Nashville, Tennessee 37219
Distributed in Canada by H. B. Fenn & Company, Ltd.
34 Nixon Rd., Bolton, Ontario L7E 1W2.

Typography by D&T/Bailey Typesetting, Inc., Nashville, Tennessee

Library of Congress Cataloging-in-Publication Data

Couch, Ernia, 1949–
    Presidential trivia / compiled by Ernie Couch.
        p.   cm.
    ISBN 1-55853-412-1
    1. Presidents—United States—Miscellanea.   1. Title.
E176.1.C796   1996   96-2523
973'.099—dc20   CIP

Printed in the United States of America
4 5 6 7 8 9 — 99 98

To
the people who choose to
participate in the great process of democracy
that selects our nation's highest servant
and to
Miss Jill and Jason
for continuing to believe
in my projects.

CONTENTS

PREFACE 9

I.   LIFE BEFORE THE PRESIDENCY 11

II. EXECUTING THE OFFICE 55

III. PRESIDENTIAL HOUSEHOLDS 93

IV. PRESIDENTIAL MISCELLANEA 141

PRESIDENTS OF THE UNITED STATES 188

PREFACE

From its rather humble beginnings as a limited administrative position in a small, newly formed nation, the office of president of the United States has grown to be the single most influential position in present-day world politics. *Presidential Trivia* is a collection of questions and answers about the individuals, with their diversified backgrounds and multi-faceted personalities, who have pursued and served in this high office. Both known and not-so-well-known facts about the lives of the presidents, their families, and the events that shaped their administrations are compiled in these pages. It is hoped that *Presidential Trivia* will encourage readers to learn more about each of the fascinating individuals who have served as president of the United States.

—ERNIE COUCH

LIFE BEFORE THE PRESIDENCY

Q. To what five-year-old White House visitor did President Grover Cleveland say, "My little man, I am making a strange wish for you—it is that you may never be president of the United States"?

A. Franklin D. Roosevelt, who was elected president four times.

Q. What name was given to Gerald Ford at birth?

A. Leslie Lynch King, Jr.

Q. What ended Dwight D. Eisenhower's football career at the U.S. Military Academy?

A. A knee injury.

Q. How many times did Rutherford B. Hayes have his horse shot out from under him while serving in the Union army during the Civil War?

A. Four.

Q. As a child, Martin Van Buren was called by what nickname?

A. "Little Mat."

Q. Although he later overcame his disability, which president suffered from habitual slobbering during his childhood and teens?

A. Andrew Jackson.

Q. Which president was born in Lamar, Missouri, on May 8, 1884?

A. Harry S. Truman.

Q. Who did William Henry Harrison offend with his blunt statements pertaining to dictatorships, which led to his recall as a diplomat in South America?

A. Simón Bolívar.

Q. In what 1951 movie did Ronald Reagan co-star with a chimpanzee?

A. *Bedtime for Bonzo.*

Q. What three presidents had previously worked as surveyors?

A. George Washington, John Adams, and Abraham Lincoln.

Q. At the outset of his presidential campaign, Grover Cleveland admitted to having had an intimate affair with, and possibly having fathered a son by, what Buffalo, New York, woman?

A. Maria Halpin.

Q. What noted politician challenged James Monroe to a duel, although it was never fought?

A. Alexander Hamilton.

Q. Which president attended Oxford University in England as a Rhodes scholar?

A. Bill Clinton.

Q. Who was the first chief executive born in a hospital?

A. Jimmy Carter (Wise Hospital, Plains, Georgia).

Q. John F. Kennedy was skipper of what naval vessel that was rammed and sunk by a Japanese destroyer on August 2, 1943?

A. PT-109.

Q. What nickname was given to Ronald Reagan as an infant by his father?

A. "Dutch."

Q. What noted author penned Benjamin Harrison's official campaign biography for the 1888 election?

A. General Lou Wallace.

Q. As a youth, Bill Clinton formed what jazz combo with two other boys?

A. Three Blind Mice.

Q. During the Spanish-American War, what did Theodore Roosevelt always carry at least six pairs of into combat?

A. Spectacles (eye glasses).

Q. What were Dwight D. Eisenhower's two favorite subjects in high school?

A. Plane geometry and history.

Q. In the summer of 1861, the Union army's Twenty-third Regiment in Ohio held in its ranks what two future presidents?

A. William McKinley and Rutherford B. Hayes.

Q. At what university was Gerald Ford a football star?

A. University of Michigan.

Q. Who was the first president born west of the Mississippi River?

A. Herbert Hoover.

Q. What "priceless gift" was in a ring presented to Theodore Roosevelt by Secretary of State John Hay on the evening before his inauguration?

A. A clipping of Abraham Lincoln's hair.

Q. During the Civil War, while Ulysses S. Grant was commanding Union troops at Vicksburg, Mississippi, a servant girl accidentally threw what personal item of Grant's into the Mississippi River?

A. His false teeth.

Q. Which president had previously worked as an assistant teacher at a New York City school for the blind?

A. Grover Cleveland.

Q. Which president was outfitted in dresses until age five by his mother?

A. Franklin D. Roosevelt.

Q. Taking advantage of the provisions of the Conscription Act of 1863, which president paid a substitute $150 to take his place in the Union army?

A. Grover Cleveland.

Q. To young Abraham Lincoln's dismay, what much beloved childhood pet became the Lincoln family's breakfast entrée?

A. His pig.

Q. Though Ronald Reagan served three years in the army during World War II, what kept him from being permitted to go into combat?

A. Poor eyesight.

Q. How much did Richard Nixon weigh at birth?

A. Eleven pounds.

Q. While in his early twenties, who became known as the "Cyclone Assemblyman" in New York state politics?

A. Theodore Roosevelt.

Q. Who absent-mindedly suggested a system whereby annual elections would be held on February 29?

A. Thomas Jefferson.

Q. Franklin D. Roosevelt's mother insisted that he call her by what title?

A. "Dear Mama."

Q. What was Woodrow Wilson's annual salary as a professor at Bryn Mawr College in Pennsylvania?

A. $1,500.

Q. Who was the first West Point graduate to become president of the United States?

A. Ulysses S. Grant.

Q. What Democratic opponent did George Bush defeat in the 1988 presidential election?

A. Michael S. Dukakis.

Q. What pirate leader, along with his men, assisted Andrew Jackson in the defense of New Orleans?

A. Jean Laffite.

Q. Although ultimately chosen by the House of Representatives as president, Thomas Jefferson tied with what other candidate in the Electoral College vote?

A. Aaron Burr.

Q. What type of part-time job did teenager Richard Nixon have with the Slippery Gulch Rodeo in Prescott, Arizona?

A. A barker for a game of chance.

Q. Seventeen-year-old George Washington secured a surveyor's assistant job helping lay out what town site in Virginia?

A. Alexandria.

Q. What was Jimmy Carter's boyhood nickname?

A. "Hot" (short for "Hot Shot").

Q. Where, on June 18, 1858, did Abraham Lincoln make his famous "House Divided" speech?

A. Springfield, Illinois.

Q. Herbert Hoover became a millionaire, but as an orphan farm boy he was paid what amount to pick potato bugs from plants.

A. One dollar per one hundred bugs.

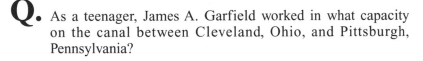

Q. As a teenager, James A. Garfield worked in what capacity on the canal between Cleveland, Ohio, and Pittsburgh, Pennsylvania?

A. Mule driver.

Q. At what age did Franklin D. Roosevelt contract polio?

A. Thirty-nine.

Q. How many crashes did George Bush survive as a navy pilot in World War II?

A. Four.

Q. What vocation had Richard Nixon's mother hoped he would pursue?

A. Quaker missionary.

Q. Where were 160 acres of land given to John Tyler as a veteran's bonus for his participation in the War of 1812?

A. Present-day Sioux City, Iowa.

Q. George Washington prominently carved his initials on what scenic natural wonder in Virginia?

A. Natural Bridge, Rockbridge County.

Q. During World War II, Gerald Ford served aboard what light aircraft carrier that participated in most of the major battles of the South Pacific?

A. USS *Monterey.*

Q. By what name was the cavalry regiment Theodore Roosevelt commanded during the Spanish-American War known?

A. The Rough Riders.

Q. Jimmy Carter graduated from what service academy?

A. The Naval Academy at Annapolis, Maryland.

Q. In what Indian conflict did Abraham Lincoln briefly serve as a captain of volunteers and as a private in a ranger company?

A. Black Hawk War.

Q. James A. Garfield rose to what military rank in the Union army during the Civil War?

A. Major general.

Q. From what institution of higher learning did John Adams receive two degrees?

A. Harvard.

Q. In what year did Dwight D. Eisenhower graduate from West Point?

A. 1915.

Q. At age nineteen, Lyndon B. Johnson joined what church?

A. Christian Church (or Disciples of Christ).

Q. In what year was Ronald Reagan first elected governor of California?

A. 1966.

Q. Upon what did teenager Andrew Jackson squander the inheritance of approximately £300 which his merchant grandfather in Ireland had left him?

A. Gambling, horse races, and cock fights.

Q. At what exclusive prep school did Franklin D. Roosevelt play football?

A. Groton.

Q. What president, in speaking of his demeanor as a child, said, "I was kind of a sissy"?

A. Harry S. Truman.

Q. What president taught school for a short time at age sixteen near Waxhaw, South Carolina?

A. Andrew Jackson.

Q. In the early 1940s, Richard Nixon was a part-owner and president of what short-lived California frozen orange juice company?

A. Citra-Frost Company.

Q. During World War I, Harry S. Truman served as the captain of what type of military unit?

A. Artillery.

Q. Abraham Lincoln's first salaried job as a store clerk paid him what amount?

A. Fifty-cents a day, plus sleeping accommodations.

Q. How old was Andrew Jackson when he was admitted to the bar in North Carolina as a lawyer?

A. Twenty.

Q. In 1962 Ronald Reagan became the host of what television western series?

A. *Death Valley Days.*

Q. Who was known for his "New Frontier" presidential nomination acceptance speech?

A. John F. Kennedy.

———◆———

Q. In addition to serving as commissioner to France, John Adams also served in the capacity of minister to what two nations?

A. Netherlands and England.

———◆———

Q. Andrew Jackson's victory over the British on January 8, 1815, came how long after the signing of the Treaty of Ghent ending the War of 1812?

A. Two weeks.

———◆———

Q. At an annual salary of $400, Benjamin Harrison served as attorney for what Indiana city?

A. Indianapolis.

———◆———

Q. As a young law student, what president broke into the dean's office at Duke University Law School?

A. Richard Nixon.

———◆———

Q. During the War of 1812, John Tyler was briefly a captain in what militia unit?

A. Charles City Rifles.

———◆———

Q. Although Andrew Jackson received ninety-nine electoral votes to John Quincy Adams's eighty-four votes in the 1824 election, what other candidate threw his support and votes to Adams, insuring Adams's victory?

A. Henry Clay.

Q. While serving as governor of Georgia, Jimmy Carter filed a detailed report as to having seen what phenomenon over Leary, Georgia, on the evening of January 6, 1969?

A. UFO (Unidentified Flying Object).

Q. Woodrow Wilson earned a Ph.D. in political science from what university in 1886?

A. Johns Hopkins University.

Q. In 1828 Martin Van Buren was elected governor of what state?

A. New York.

Q. At what age did Harry S. Truman start wearing glasses?

A. Six.

Q. During the election of 1828, supporters of John Quincy Adams circulated what anti-Andrew Jackson publication criticizing Jackson's execution of six mutineers during the War of 1812?

A. The "Coffin Handbill."

Q. Where, at age sixteen, did Andrew Johnson open his first tailor shop?

A. Laurens Court House, South Carolina.

Q. What presidential candidate's election campaign was known for the slogan "Tippecanoe and Tyler too"?

A. William Henry Harrison.

Q. Who was the first president to be born in a log cabin?

A. Andrew Jackson.

———◆———

Q. During the Mexican War, a decisive victory over what general at Buena Vista, Mexico, sky-rocketed Zachary Taylor to the status of national hero?

A. General Antonio López de Santa Anna.

———◆———

Q. Port Conway, Virginia, is the birthplace of what early president?

A. James Madison.

———◆———

Q. Where did six-year-old Harry S. Truman first meet his future wife, Bess, who was at the time five years old?

A. Sunday school.

———◆———

Q. During his navy career, Jimmy Carter had seven years of duty on what type of vessel?

A. Submarine.

———◆———

Q. At what engagement with the British during the Revolutionary War was James Monroe severely wounded?

A. Battle of Trenton.

———◆———

Q. What disease did Andrew Jackson contract while a prisoner-of-war at Camden, South Carolina?

A. Smallpox.

Q. Who pursued a political journalism career and published articles under such pen names as "Publicola," "Marcellus," and "Columbus"?

A. John Quincy Adams.

Q. What Republican campaign song played a role in the election of Benjamin Harrison?

A. "Grandfather's Hat Fits Ben."

Q. What president was born in the Dutch settlement of Kinderhook, New York, on December 5, 1782?

A. Martin Van Buren.

Q. As a youth, Warren G. Harding played what brass instrument in the local band at Caledonia, Ohio?

A. Cornet.

Q. In what territory did Zachary Taylor become commander of all United States forces in 1838?

A. Florida Territory.

Q. Young prisoner-of-war Andrew Jackson was slashed with a sword for refusing what task from a British soldier?

A. Cleaning his boots.

Q. Who said of Ulysses S. Grant, "[I] have never found Grant's superior as a general"?

A. General Robert E. Lee.

Q. What profession did William Henry Harrison's father want William to pursue?

A. Physician.

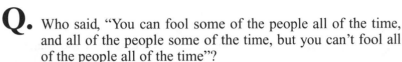

Q. Who said, "You can fool some of the people all of the time, and all of the people some of the time, but you can't fool all of the people all of the time"?

A. Abraham Lincoln (1856).

Q. In 1902 Woodrow Wilson became president of what institution of higher learning?

A. Princeton University.

Q. Following a complete mental and emotional collapse at age twenty-four, Warren G. Harding received treatment at the sanitarium of what noted physician in Battle Creek, Michigan?

A. Dr. J. P. Kellogg.

Q. What New York state political office did Martin Van Buren assume in 1816?

A. Attorney general.

Q. When Franklin D. Roosevelt was born, what name did Franklin's father want to assign to his new son?

A. Isaac.

Q. James K. Polk's partisan rhetoric and small stature earned him what nickname?

A. "Napoleon of the Stump."

Q. Long before recycling for ecology's sake came into vogue, Herbert Hoover, as a boy, collected what type of material to generate money?

A. Scrap iron.

Q. Which president was born in Point Pleasant, Ohio, on April 27, 1822?

A. Ulysses S. Grant.

Q. Where did James Madison attend college?

A. College of New Jersey (now Princeton University).

Q. Where was Bill Clinton born?

A. Julie Chester Hospital, Hope, Arkansas.

Q. Where was Zachary Taylor stationed in 1841 as commander of the Second Department of the Western Division of the U.S. Army?

A. Fort Smith, Arkansas.

Q. Which president, at birth, had to be administered mouth-to-mouth resuscitation, having entered the world stupored from his mother after she received an overdose of chloroform?

A. Franklin D. Roosevelt.

Q. How many consecutive terms did James K. Polk serve in the U.S. House of Representatives?

A. Seven.

Q. Which president was born in Charles City County, Virginia, on March 29, 1790?

A. John Tyler.

Q. At age thirteen, Andrew Jackson joined what military group?

A. South Carolina mounted militia.

Q. At what two Ohio newspapers did teenager Warren G. Harding work prior to borrowing $300 to purchase the *Marion Star*?

A. *Caledonia Argus* and *Marion Democratic Mirror.*

Q. By his own account, how many people did Ronald Reagan save from drowning during the six or seven summers he served as a lifeguard near his hometown in Illinois?

A. Seventy-seven.

Q. While serving in the U.S. Senate, Martin Van Buren became a leading figure in the fight to abolish what grounds for imprisonment?

A. Debt.

Q. Though he never graduated, William Henry Harrison entered what institution of higher learning in 1787?

A. Hampden-Sydney College.

Q. In response to insulting remarks about Rachel Jackson and himself, who did Andrew Jackson kill in a duel on the Red River in Kentucky?

A. Charles Dickinson of Nashville, Tennessee.

Q. Which chief executive was born on February 6, 1911, in a rented apartment above a bakery in Tampico, Illinois?

A. Ronald Reagan.

Q. How old was George Washington when his father, Augustine Washington, died?

A. Eleven.

Q. Prior to becoming the forty-second president of the United States, Bill Clinton was governor of what state?

A. Arkansas.

Q. Zachary Taylor was born near what Virginia town on November 24, 1784?

A. Barboursville.

Q. How many nationally televised debates did John F. Kennedy and Richard Nixon engage in during the 1960 presidential campaign?

A. Four.

Q. As a teenager, Millard Fillmore was apprenticed to what type of craftsman?

A. Clothmaker.

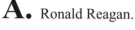

Q. What name did Andrew Jackson give to the plantation he purchased near Nashville, Tennessee, in 1804?

A. The Hermitage.

Q. In his youth, what president received a ten-dollar tip for retrieving a swimmer's false teeth from the bottom of the Rock River in Illinois?

A. Ronald Reagan.

Q. Where was Herbert Hoover born?

A. West Branch, Iowa.

Q. As a U.S. senator, Martin Van Buren proposed, but failed to pass, a ban on the importation of what demographic group into Florida?

A. Slaves.

Q. Having learned the alphabet at age two, how old was Lyndon B. Johnson when his mother, Rebekah Baines, taught him to read?

A. Four.

Q. Although Benjamin Harrison first attended Farmers' College, from what Ohio university did he graduate in 1852?

A. Miami University.

Q. Which president, as a youth, worked as a court crier?

A. Benjamin Harrison.

Q. In what 1937 motion picture did Ronald Reagan make his screen debut?

A. *Love Is in the Air.*

Q. How much did Bill Clinton weigh at birth?

A. Six pounds.

———◆———

Q. Under whom did Franklin Pierce serve during the Mexican War and later run against for the presidency?

A. General Winfield Scott.

———◆———

Q. In 1832 who negotiated with the court of Czar Nicholas I in securing the United States' first trade treaty with Russia?

A. James Buchanan.

———◆———

Q. During the French and Indian War, George Washington ordered the body of what deceased general to be buried in the middle of a wagon trail to protect it from desecration by the enemy?

A. General Edward Braddock.

———◆———

Q. James Buchanan served in what capacity within James K. Polk's cabinet?

A. Secretary of state.

———◆———

Q. Who was the first candidate Ronald Reagan voted for in a presidential election?

A. Franklin D. Roosevelt (1932).

———◆———

Q. In the early 1950s, what title was applied to Richard Nixon that followed him through the remainder of his political career?

A. "Tricky Dick."

Q. As a boy, Lyndon B. Johnson ran an ad in the family-owned-and-operated newspaper to advertise what personal enterprise?

A. His bootblack business.

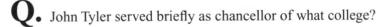

Q. James K. Polk was born near what North Carolina town on November 2, 1795?

A. Pineville.

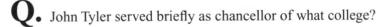

Q. At what radio station did Ronald Reagan secure his first employment as a sportscaster?

A. WOC, Davenport, Iowa.

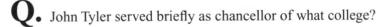

Q. Andrew Jackson became the provisional governor of what territory in 1821?

A. Florida.

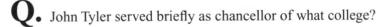

Q. John Tyler served briefly as chancellor of what college?

A. William and Mary College.

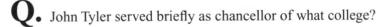

Q. While attending Union College in Schenectady, New York, Chester Arthur, as a prank, assisted in throwing the school's bell in what waterway?

A. The Erie Canal.

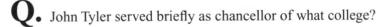

Q. Who did President Andrew Jackson appoint as minister to Russia in 1831?

A. James Buchanan.

Q. James K. Polk was elected governor of what state in 1839?

A. Tennessee.

Q. As a young man, which president's first elected post was to serve as a member of the Committee of Safety for Orange County, Virginia?

A. James Madison.

Q. Dwight D. Eisenhower served as president of what university from 1948 to 1950?

A. Columbia University.

Q. Where did George Washington, Andrew Jackson, Martin Van Buren, Zachary Taylor, Millard Fillmore, Abraham Lincoln, Andrew Johnson, Grover Cleveland, and Harry S. Truman all attend college?

A. Nowhere.

Q. What rank did Franklin Pierce ultimately attain during the Mexican War?

A. Brigadier general.

Q. In order to facilitate his commercial trading ventures, as a young entrepreneur, Andrew Jackson signed a statement of allegiance to what European power?

A. Spain.

Q. Where did Harry S. Truman receive his basic training while in the U.S. Army?

A. Camp Doniphan, Fort Sill, Oklahoma.

Q. While serving as a navy pilot during World War II, which future president flew fifty-eight combat missions?

A. George Bush.

Q. In 1846 who became the first chancellor of the University of Buffalo in New York?

A. Millard Fillmore.

Q. What was the name of the family plantation on which William Henry Harrison was born in Charles City County, Virginia?

A. Berkeley.

Q. Where was George Bush born?

A. Milton, Massachusetts.

Q. As a lawyer, what was the largest fee Abraham Lincoln ever received for successfully defending a client?

A. $5,000 (from the Illinois Central Railroad).

Q. What was William Henry Harrison's first political office?

A. Secretary of the Northwest Territory.

Q. James K. Polk was the oldest of how many children in his family?

A. Ten.

Q. In 1831 Millard Fillmore became a charter member of what church in Buffalo, New York?

A. The Unitarian Church.

Q. What was the total length of Abraham Lincoln's formal education?

A. Less than one year.

Q. Where was George Washington born?

A. Pope's Creek Farm (now Wakefield), Westmoreland County, Virginia.

Q. What New York senator declined his party's nomination to be James K. Polk's running mate?

A. Silas Wright.

Q. In what Arkansas town did Bill Clinton spend most of his childhood and teenage years?

A. Hot Springs.

Q. During the Illinois senatorial campaign of 1858, debates with what eminent senator brought Abraham Lincoln to national attention?

A. Stephen A. Douglas.

Q. Outnumbered by Mexican forces at least three to one, Zachary Taylor and his troops won a victory in what February 22 and 23, 1847, military engagement?

A. The Battle of Buena Vista.

Q. The Illinois State Republican Convention applied what nickname to Abraham Lincoln?

A. "The Railsplitter."

Q. Because of his diminutive stature, what nickname was given to Benjamin Harrison by the men who served under him during the Civil War?

A. "Little Ben."

Q. Who was the first elected delegate to Congress from the Northwest Territory?

A. William Henry Harrison.

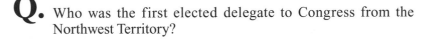

Q. Prior to serving as governor, what other public office did Bill Clinton hold in Arkansas?

A. State attorney general (1977-79).

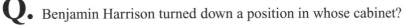

Q. While attending Amherst College, what was Calvin Coolidge's worst subject?

A. Physics.

Q. Benjamin Harrison turned down a position in whose cabinet?

A. James A. Garfield's.

Q. Ronald Reagan played what character in the 1940 motion picture *Knute Rockne—All American*?

A. George Gipp.

Q. Who were Richard Nixon's two major opponents in the 1968 presidential election?

A. Hubert H. Humphrey (Democrat) and George Wallace (Independent).

———◆———

Q. Which president was born on the Fourth of July?

A. Calvin Coolidge (1872).

———◆———

Q. From whom did Richard Nixon's mother derive his first name?

A. King Richard I ("the Lion-Hearted").

———◆———

Q. On what ballot did the Democratic Party finally select Franklin Pierce as their presidential candidate for the 1852 election?

A. Forty-ninth.

———◆———

Q. At what college did Woodrow Wilson coach football?

A. Bryn Mawr College, Pennsylvania.

———◆———

Q. In 1855 who successfully represented Lizzie Jennings in a landmark case which led to the desegregation of public transportation in New York City?

A. Chester A. Arthur.

———◆———

Q. At a 1963 White House reception with participants in the American Legion-sponsored Boys' Nation program, President John F. Kennedy shook hands with what teenaged future president?

A. Bill Clinton.

Q. Where did Franklin Pierce open his first law office?

A. Concord, New Hampshire.

———◆———

Q. As a teenager, Theodore Roosevelt climbed what wonder of the ancient world?

A. The Great Pyramid at Giza, Egypt.

———◆———

Q. While serving as governor of the Indiana Territory, William Henry Harrison ordered that Indians within the territory be inoculated against what disease?

A. Smallpox.

———◆———

Q. What college did Franklin Pierce enter in 1820?

A. Bowdoin College.

———◆———

Q. During Warren G. Harding's 1920 presidential campaign, what white supremacist published materials claiming Harding's great-great-grandfather to have been of West Indian black heritage?

A. William Estabrook Chanceller.

———◆———

Q. Who claimed to have had an affair with Dwight D. Eisenhower while serving as the general's driver, secretary, and aide during World War II?

A. Kay Summersby.

———◆———

Q. Franklin Pierce moved from last in his class during his second year in college to what ranking at graduation?

A. Third.

Q. At age seventeen, Zachary Taylor swam back and forth across what major river?

A. Ohio River.

Q. From 1903 to 1905, Warren G. Harding held what state office in Ohio?

A. Lieutenant governor.

Q. In his late teens, which president worked as a clerk in the mailroom of the *Kansas City Star*?

A. Harry S. Truman.

Q. What noted entertainer composed and nationally performed a campaign song for Warren G. Harding's presidential bid?

A. Al Jolson.

Q. John Tyler served as governor of what state from 1825 to 1827?

A. Virginia.

Q. At what battle, near present-day Lafayette, Indiana, did William Henry Harrison lead his outnumbered militia to a victory over Indian forces on November 7, 1811?

A. The Battle of Tippecanoe.

Q. James M. Cox, who ran against Warren G. Harding in the 1920 presidential race, had what New York native as his vice-presidential running mate?

A. Franklin D. Roosevelt.

Q. *Arkansas Democrat-Gazette* newspaper columnist Paul Greenberg saddled Bill Clinton with what nickname?

A. "Slick Willie."

Q. In 1848 what anti-slavery party nominated Martin Van Buren as a presidential candidate?

A. Free-Soil Party.

Q. Which president, at age seventeen, underwent a gall bladder operation without anesthesia?

A. James K. Polk.

Q. While serving as U.S. senator from Ohio, Warren G. Harding was present for what percentage of roll-call votes in the Senate?

A. Less than one-third.

Q. What years did Bill Clinton serve as the governor of Arkansas?

A. 1979-81 and 1983-92.

Q. To what military rank was Dwight D. Eisenhower promoted in December 1945?

A. Five-star general.

Q. In 1833 Abraham Lincoln applied for and received what type of license?

A. Saloon license.

Q. What Pennsylvania lawyer was James K. Polk's running mate in the 1844 election?

A. George M. Dallas.

Q. What incumbent defeated Richard Nixon in the 1962 California gubernatorial election?

A. Edmund G. "Pat" Brown.

Q. What was the main campaign slogan for Lyndon B. Johnson in the 1964 presidential election?

A. "All the Way with LBJ."

Q. At age fifteen, Warren G. Harding entered what college at Iberia, Ohio?

A. Central Ohio College.

Q. The National Music Company of Chicago published what song alluding to the sex scandal that plagued Grover Cleveland's first presidential campaign?

A. "Ma! Ma! Where's My Pa?"

Q. In what mid-1950s motion picture did both Ronald and Nancy Reagan appear?

A. *Hellcats of the Navy.*

Q. Although he did not accept the appointment, Abraham Lincoln was offered the governorship of what U.S. territory in 1849?

A. Oregon.

Q. As boys, which two presidents were indentured laborers?

A. Millard Fillmore and Andrew Johnson.

Q. What 1976-77 director of the CIA became president of the United States?

A. George Bush.

Q. Bill Clinton taught at what university from 1973 to 1976?

A. University of Arkansas, Fayetteville.

Q. What president earned thirty dollars per month teaching school at White Schoolhouse near Marion, Ohio?

A. Warren G. Harding.

Q. In 1828 William Henry Harrison became the first U.S. minister to what South American country?

A. Colombia.

Q. What former Miss Europe and film actress with high Nazi connections dated John F. Kennedy in 1941 and 1942?

A. Inga Arvad.

Q. Following World War I, Harry S. Truman, along with his partner Eddie Jacobson, established what type of business in Kansas City?

A. A haberdashery.

Q. As a young man, what president appeared in a 1940 clothes-modeling spread in *Look* magazine and later on the cover of *Cosmopolitan*?

A. Gerald Ford.

◆

Q. Prior to a formal declaration of war with Mexico, Zachary Taylor and some 4,000 U.S. troops defeated Mexican forces at what two Rio Grande sites?

A. Palo Alto and Resaca de la Palma.

◆

Q. The slogan "Keep the ball rolling" originated during whose Whig presidential campaign?

A. William Henry Harrison.

◆

Q. Giving in to her husband's wishes, Warren G. Harding's mother agreed not to name the future president Winfield but still insisted on calling him by what nickname?

A. "Winnie."

◆

Q. Which president was born at Cove Gap near Mercersburg, Pennsylvania, in 1791?

A. James Buchanan.

◆

Q. At age eighteen, James Madison received what military rank?

A. Lieutenant.

◆

Q. As a young man, which president worked as a park ranger at Yellowstone National Park?

A. Gerald Ford (1936).

Q. What disease left nine-year-old Harry S. Truman with a paralyzed leg and arm for several months?

A. Diphtheria.

Q. Following the burning of Washington, D.C., in addition to continuing to serve as secretary of state, James Madison held what other cabinet position for the duration of the War of 1812?

A. Secretary of war.

Q. On what date was William Henry Harrison born?

A. February 9, 1773.

Q. What did Ronald Reagan collect as a youth?

A. Birds' eggs and butterflies.

Q. At age fourteen, who served as the private secretary of America's first resident diplomat in Russia?

A. John Quincy Adams.

Q. At the urging of New York governor Thomas Dewey, who did Dwight D. Eisenhower select as his vice-presidential running mate in the 1952 election?

A. Richard Nixon.

Q. For a while in the mid-1920s, Harry S. Truman sold memberships to what organization?

A. Kansas City Automobile Club.

Q. What book, derived from John F. Kennedy's senior thesis at Harvard University, became a bestseller in 1940?

A. *While England Slept.*

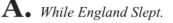

Q. What was Dwight D. Eisenhower's most famous slogan during his 1952 presidential campaign?

A. "I like Ike."

Q. As a young man, which president worked as a janitor and teacher at schools in the Ohio towns of Warrensville Heights and Blue Rock?

A. James A. Garfield.

Q. Who was President Harry S. Truman's vice-presidential running mate in the 1948 election?

A. Alben William Barkley.

Q. A former slave was the common-law wife of which president's vice-presidential running mate?

A. Martin Van Buren (V.P. Richard M. Johnson).

Q. Where did Dwight D. Eisenhower attend high school?

A. Abilene High School, Abilene, Kansas.

Q. Who was Abraham Lincoln's vice-presidential running mate in the 1860 election?

A. Hannibal Hamlin of Maine.

Q. Where was Dwight D. Eisenhower born?

A. Denison, Texas.

Q. What years did Harry S. Truman serve as U.S. senator from Missouri?

A. 1935-1945.

Q. What rank in the Boy Scouts of America did Gerald Ford attain?

A. Eagle Scout.

Q. In 1919, while serving as governor of Massachusetts, Calvin Coolidge received national attention and local praise for his handling of a strike by what group of public servants in Boston?

A. Police.

Q. At the pleading of fifteen-year-old Dwight D. Eisenhower, his parents chose not to allow a physician to carry out what treatment for blood poisoning in his leg?

A. Amputation.

Q. Who edited President William Henry Harrison's lengthy inaugural address?

A. Daniel Webster.

Q. What 688-acre ranch, in the mountains east of Santa Barbara, California, did Ronald Reagan purchase in 1974?

A. Rancho de Cielo.

Q. What was Bill Clinton's name at birth?

A. William Jefferson Blythe.

◆

Q. At age seven, Herbert Hoover spent several months living with his uncle on what Oklahoma Territory Indian reservation?

A. Osage Reservation, Pawhuska.

◆

Q. While attending the U.S. Naval Academy, Jimmy Carter received verbal abuse and mild physical punishment for refusing an upperclassman's order to sing what Civil War song?

A. "Marching through Georgia."

◆

Q. Prior to becoming president, who served as governor of New York from 1929 to 1933?

A. Franklin D. Roosevelt.

◆

Q. In April 1862 General Ulysses S. Grant and his troops engaged in what bloody battle near Pittsburg Landing on the Tennessee River?

A. The Battle of Shiloh.

◆

Q. Although noted as a great army general, where did Dwight D. Eisenhower first apply to further his military education?

A. U.S. Naval Academy.

◆

Q. Who was Zachary Taylor's running mate on the Whig ticket during the 1848 election?

A. Millard Fillmore.

Q. During his freshman year at Stanford, what position did Herbert Hoover play on the university's baseball team?

A. Shortstop.

Q. Which chief executive bore a scar above his right eye which he received in a fight with would-be thieves?

A. Abraham Lincoln.

Q. Who served as governor of Tennessee from 1853 to 1857 and again as military governor of the state from 1862 to 1864?

A. Andrew Johnson.

Q. Where was John F. Kennedy born?

A. Brookline, Massachusetts.

Q. In the 1880 election, what Democratic opponent did James A. Garfield defeat by a narrow margin of 9,464 popular votes?

A. Winfield S. Hancock.

Q. In April 1951, Dwight D. Eisenhower assumed his duties as supreme commander of what multinational alliance?

A. North Atlantic Treaty Organization (NATO).

Q. What was the name of Herbert Hoover's dog, which was featured in his presidential campaign promotional materials to help create a warmer image?

A. King Tut.

Q. In Franklin D. Roosevelt's 1932 presidential bid, what was his campaign theme song?

A. "Happy Days Are Here Again."

———◆———

Q. What was the name of the airplane used by Ronald Reagan during the 1980 presidential campaign?

A. *Leadership 1980.*

———◆———

Q. While courting his future wife, Lucretia Rudolph, James A. Garfield was also dating what other young lady?

A. Rebecca J. "Rancie" Selleck.

———◆———

Q. As the first cabinet member from west of the Mississippi River, who did President Abraham Lincoln appoint to the post of attorney general?

A. Edward Bates.

———◆———

Q. During the 1952 election, vice-presidential candidate Richard Nixon's sentimental statement about what family pet neutralized accusations of a secret campaign slush fund?

A. Checkers, the Nixons' cocker spaniel.

———◆———

Q. What religious denomination did James A. Garfield join in 1850?

A. Disciples of Christ.

———◆———

Q. Who was the first president to be born in the twentieth century?

A. John F. Kennedy.

Q. In the mid-1850s, Ulysses S. Grant supplemented his meager farm income by selling what commodity in St. Louis, Missouri?

A. Wood.

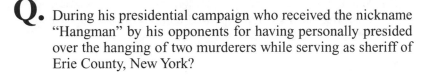

Q. During his presidential campaign who received the nickname "Hangman" by his opponents for having personally presided over the hanging of two murderers while serving as sheriff of Erie County, New York?

A. Grover Cleveland.

Q. As a young man, Rutherford B. Hayes contended with what phobia?

A. A fear of going insane.

Q. What English teacher did President Jimmy Carter pay tribute to in his inaugural speech?

A. Miss Julia Coleman.

Q. Which president was named for the physician who delivered him?

A. Chester A. Arthur (for Dr. Chester Abell).

Q. In 1954 John F. Kennedy underwent what type of surgery?

A. Spinal fusion.

Q. Herbert and Lou Hoover were residents of what Chinese city during the Boxer Rebellion of 1900?

A. Tientsin.

Q. How long did Lyndon B. Johnson's parents wait after his birth before naming him?

A. Three months.

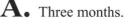

Q. What twentieth-century president was widely criticized for reneging on his often repeated campaign pledge, "Read my lips: No new taxes"?

A. George Bush.

Q. In what two subjects did Ronald Reagan major while attending Eureka College in Illinois?

A. Economics and sociology.

Q. As a boy, what was George Washington's favorite subject in school?

A. Arithmetic.

Q. Who served as chairman of the Republican National Committee in 1973-74?

A. George Bush.

Q. What left Jimmy Carter with a permanently crooked finger?

A. Cotton gin accident.

Q. Following the death of his wife, Hannah, in 1819, Martin Van Buren reportedly courted and proposed to Ellen Randolph, the granddaughter of what former president?

A. Thomas Jefferson.

Q. Who was the first president to have been born in Texas?

A. Dwight D. Eisenhower.

———◆———

Q. What was the name of the first submarine on which Jimmy Carter served in 1948?

A. USS *Pomfret.*

———◆———

Q. What was the name of Herbert Hoover's vice-presidential running mate who was half Native American and at times referred to as "Indian Charlie"?

A. Charles Curtis.

———◆———

Q. John F. Kennedy was awarded a Pulitzer Prize for what literary work?

A. *Profiles in Courage.*

———◆———

Q. George Bush served as the chief U.S. liaison to what nation in 1974-75?

A. China.

———◆———

Q. In 1751, while on his only foreign trip, George Washington contracted what disease on the island of Barbados?

A. Smallpox.

———◆———

Q. Who was Ronald Reagan's high school and college sweetheart?

A. Margaret "Mugs" Cleaver.

Q. Who came forward during the 1992 presidential campaign to claim that she had been engaged in a twelve-year affair with Bill Clinton?

A. Gennifer Flowers.

Q. What military decoration did George Washington introduce in 1782?

A. Order of the Purple Heart.

Q. Who was the only nineteenth-century president born in New Jersey?

A. Grover Cleveland.

Q. Who was given the title "Hero of Appomattox"?

A. Ulysses S. Grant.

Q. Prior to becoming president, Jimmy Carter appeared on what television game show?

A. *What's My Line?*

Q. While he was serving as governor of California, how long did Ronald Reagan and his family live in the governor's mansion in Sacramento?

A. Four months.

Q. Where was John Adams born?

A. Braintree (now Quincy), Massachusetts.

Q. As a World War II naval pilot, what name did George Bush assign to all of the aircraft that he captained?

A. *Barbara.*

Q. What was the amount of the trust fund John F. Kennedy received from his father for his twenty-first birthday?

A. One million dollars.

Q. To what position with the state government of New York was Millard Fillmore elected in 1847?

A. Comptroller.

Q. Where on March 9, 1831, did Abraham Lincoln make his first political speech?

A. New Salem, Illinois.

EXECUTING THE OFFICE

Q. What chief executive was arrested, and his carriage and horse impounded, for speeding on a Washington street?

A. Ulysses S. Grant.

Q. On April 14, 1910, William H. Taft became the first president to throw out the season-opening pitch for professional baseball at what stadium?

A. Griffith Stadium, Washington, D.C.

Q. Who was not only the first U.S. president to win a Nobel Peace Prize, but also the first American to be so honored?

A. Theodore Roosevelt.

Q. What two foreign leaders did President Jimmy Carter invite to Camp David for a series of meetings that eventually led to a peace treaty between Egypt and Israel?

A. Anwar el-Sadat and Menachem Begin.

Q. Who was foiled in his attempt to assassinate President Andrew Jackson on January 30, 1835, when each of his two pistols misfired?

A. Richard Lawrence.

Q. Who was the first incumbent president to meet with a pontiff?

A. Lyndon B. Johnson (1966 with Pope Paul VI).

Q. In his 1984 re-election, President Ronald Reagan set a record with how many electoral votes?

A. 525 (to Walter Mondale's 13).

Q. During whose administration did seven of the fifteen slave states secede from the Union?

A. James Buchanan's.

Q. Suffering from a muscle spasm brought on by an earlier three-hour handshaking session, Abraham Lincoln dropped his pen on his first attempt to sign what famous document?

A. Emancipation Proclamation.

Q. Which president referred to himself as "the hardest working man in the country"?

A. James K. Polk.

Q. In 1970 President Richard Nixon made what entertainer an honorary special agent in the administration's war on drugs?

A. Elvis Presley.

Q. President Abraham Lincoln established the Secret Service in an attempt to curtail the activities of what criminal element?

A. Counterfeiters.

Q. Between which president's first and second terms was the annual presidential salary raised from $25,000 to $50,000?

A. Ulysses S. Grant's.

◆

Q. Which presidents required that questions from the press be submitted in writing in advance?

A. Warren G. Harding, Calvin Coolidge, and Herbert Hoover.

◆

Q. Who said his administration would be "cussed and discussed for years to come"?

A. Harry S. Truman.

◆

Q. What play was President Abraham Lincoln attending at Ford's Theatre when he was shot on the evening of April 14, 1865?

A. *Our American Cousin.*

◆

Q. In addition to the District of Columbia, what was the only state not to cast its electoral votes for President Ronald Reagan in 1984?

A. Minnesota.

◆

Q. The longest presidential inaugural address in the nation's history, comprising 8,445 words, was given by which president?

A. William Henry Harrison, who caught pneumonia while giving the speech and died less than two months later.

◆

Q. President Richard Nixon commuted the prison sentence of what noted labor boss in 1971?

A. Jimmy Hoffa.

Q. During the Warren G. Harding administration, newspaper reporter Judson Welliver became the first person to provide what service to a president?

A. Speechwriting.

Q. Where did Theodore Roosevelt travel in 1906, making him the first president to leave the United States while in office?

A. Panama Canal Zone.

Q. What 1941 event did President Franklin D. Roosevelt refer to as "a date that will live in infamy"?

A. The Japanese bombing of Pearl Harbor, Hawaii.

Q. Who served as vice president in both the first and second administrations of George Washington?

A. John Adams.

Q. During whose administration did the first diplomatic representatives from Japan come to the United States?

A. James Buchanan's.

Q. Who did President Franklin Pierce select to serve as secretary of war in his administration?

A. Jefferson Davis.

Q. William McKinley usually refused gifts while in the White House but did accept what 78-pound, flag-wrapped gift from admirers in Georgia?

A. A large watermelon.

Q. What agency did President Warren G. Harding create in 1921 with regard to government spending guidelines?

A. Bureau of the Budget.

———◆———

Q. To whom did President Calvin Coolidge present the Distinguished Flying Cross on June 11, 1927?

A. Charles A. Lindbergh.

———◆———

Q. Which president signed the act creating the Corporation for Public Broadcasting?

A. Lyndon B. Johnson (November 7, 1967).

———◆———

Q. During the winter of 1863-64, President Abraham Lincoln contracted what often-fatal disease?

A. Smallpox.

———◆———

Q. In 1833 who became the first president to ride on a railroad train?

A. Andrew Jackson.

———◆———

Q. On March 30, 1981, what mentally deranged would-be-assassin shot and seriously wounded President Ronald Reagan in an attempt to impress screen actress Jodie Foster?

A. John W. Hinckley, Jr.

———◆———

Q. Who cast the determining "not guilty" vote that cleared President Andrew Johnson of charges in his impeachment hearing before the Senate?

A. Senator Edmund Ross of Kansas.

Q. Who was the first chief executive to have his oath of office administered to him by the chief justice of the U.S. Supreme Court?

A. John Adams.

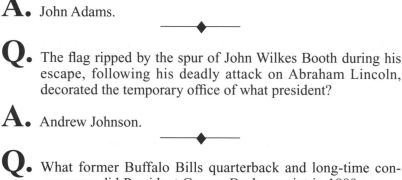

Q. The flag ripped by the spur of John Wilkes Booth during his escape, following his deadly attack on Abraham Lincoln, decorated the temporary office of what president?

A. Andrew Johnson.

Q. What former Buffalo Bills quarterback and long-time congressman did President George Bush appoint in 1989 as secretary of housing and urban development?

A. Jack Kemp.

Q. Who was the first president to use an automobile in an inaugural parade?

A. Warren G. Harding.

Q. Which president compared the executive office to "riding a tiger"?

A. Harry S. Truman.

Q. During World War II, President Franklin D. Roosevelt's wheelchair was equipped with what special piece of protective equipment?

A. A gas mask.

Q. At the time of President Abraham Lincoln's assassination, what was the only currency in his pockets?

A. A five-dollar Confederate note.

Q. How many miles did President John Quincy Adams walk each morning before addressing the day's agenda?

A. Four.

Q. President Ronald Reagan sent U.S. troops into what tiny Caribbean island nation in 1983 to squelch a leftist military coup?

A. Grenada.

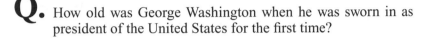

Q. How old was George Washington when he was sworn in as president of the United States for the first time?

A. Fifty-seven.

Q. A suggestion in a letter from what eleven-year-old girl from Westfield, New York, led to Abraham Lincoln's growing a beard?

A. Grace Bedell.

Q. What large animals did the king of Siam present to President James Buchanan as a gift?

A. A herd of elephants.

Q. George Washington's second inauguration was held on March 4, 1793, at what site?

A. Federal Hall, Philadelphia.

Q. In 1975 President Gerald Ford signed legislation to bail out what financially strapped city?

A. New York City.

Q. During Franklin Pierce's administration, how many night-watchmen served as the only security at the White House?

A. Two.

Q. In his re-election bid of 1812, James Madison defeated what New York City mayor?

A. DeWitt Clinton.

Q. Who did President Ronald Reagan appoint in 1981 as the first woman member of the U.S. Supreme Court?

A. Sandra Day O'Connor.

Q. In 1977 President Jimmy Carter signed into law legislation which banned the dumping of what substance into the ocean?

A. Raw sewage.

Q. What Republican presidential candidate ran unsuccessfully against Franklin D. Roosevelt in the 1940 election?

A. Wendell Willkie.

Q. Who was Jimmy Carter's vice-presidential running mate in the 1976 and 1980 elections?

A. Walter F. Mondale.

Q. What conflict did the Federalists refer to as "Mr. Madison's War"?

A. The War of 1812.

Q. In 1831 the U.S. Senate refused to confirm Andrew Jackson's appointment of Martin Van Buren as minister to what nation?

A. Great Britain.

Q. In 1880 Rutherford B. Hayes became the first president to acquire what item of office equipment for the White House?

A. Typewriter.

Q. At his first inauguration, what words did George Washington add at the end of his oath of office administered by Robert R. Livingston of New York?

A. "So help me God!"

Q. In 1979 President Jimmy Carter appointed a commission to investigate an accident at what nuclear power plant?

A. Three Mile Island, Pennsylvania.

Q. Slightly over two months into his only term, President Martin Van Buren was faced with what national financial disaster?

A. The Panic of 1837.

Q. During his term in office, which president underwent oral surgery that resulted in the removal of his upper left jawbone?

A. Grover Cleveland.

Q. On his last day in office, Andrew Jackson established diplomatic relations with what country?

A. Republic of Texas.

Q. In 1890 President Benjamin Harrison signed what bill creating the nation's first anti-trust law?

A. Sherman Anti-Trust Act.

———◆———

Q. In 1985 what Caribbean leader referred to President Ronald Reagan as "a madman, an imbecile and a bum"?

A. Fidel Castro of Cuba.

———◆———

Q. Although his father had been a Baptist minister, President Chester Arthur attended what church in Washington, D.C.?

A. St. John's Episcopal.

———◆———

Q. In 1921 President Warren G. Harding announced to Congress that the United States would not be participating in what multi-national organization?

A. The League of Nations.

———◆———

Q. Who was the first president to have his voice recorded?

A. Theodore Roosevelt.

———◆———

Q. What published directive did Andrew Jackson issue to government agents on July 11, 1836, instructing that only gold or silver be accepted for payment on public land purchases?

A. Specie Circular.

———◆———

Q. What two Puerto Rican nationalists attempted to assassinate President Harry S. Truman on November 1, 1950?

A. Oscar Collazo and Griselio Torresola.

Q. Just prior to leaving office, President Benjamin Harrison attempted, and failed, to push a treaty through the Senate that would have made what island sovereignty a territory of the United States?

A. Hawaii.

Q. What mode of transportation did William Henry Harrison choose for his inaugural parade?

A. Horseback.

Q. Who ran against James Monroe in his 1820 re-election bid?

A. No one.

Q. What vegetable did President George Bush ban from the menu of Air Force One?

A. Broccoli.

Q. During George Washington's first term, who did he appoint as secretary of state?

A. Thomas Jefferson.

Q. Warren G. Harding's administration was rocked by what scandal involving national oil reserves in Wyoming?

A. Teapot Dome Scandal.

Q. On May 11, 1846, President James K. Polk asked Congress to declare war on what country?

A. Mexico.

Q. By proclamation of President Abraham Lincoln, April 30, 1863, was set aside for what purpose?

A. "A day of national humiliation, fasting, and prayer."

———◆———

Q. Who was the first president to have a telephone installed on his desk in his White House office?

A. Herbert Hoover (1929).

———◆———

Q. Who did President Zachary Taylor appoint in 1849 as the first secretary of the interior?

A. Thomas Ewing.

———◆———

Q. Who ordered that the flag of the United States be flown over the White House and government buildings?

A. Benjamin Harrison.

———◆———

Q. What years did George Washington serve as president of the United States?

A. 1789-1797.

Q. Which president, as a chubby toddler, was nicknamed "Fatty McGee McGaw" by his father?

A. George Bush.

Q. Although later acquitted, what member of President Ronald Reagan's administration became the first secretary of labor to be indicted while serving as a cabinet member?

A. Raymond J. Donovan.

Q. Who urged Franklin Pierce to resign the Senate in 1842 and leave Washington?

A. His wife, Jane.

———◆———

Q. President Gerald Ford had a bust of what former president placed in the Oval Office?

A. Harry S. Truman.

———◆———

Q. Aboard what naval vessel did President John Tyler narrowly miss death from an explosion during the test firing of a new supercannon named "the Peacemaker"?

A. USS *Princeton.*

———◆———

Q. What name was given to a group of laws pertaining to the slavery issue that were signed into law by Millard Fillmore two months after assuming the presidency?

A. The Compromise of 1850 (the California Compromise).

———◆———

Q. What real estate investment scandal dogged Bill and Hillary Rodham Clinton?

A. Whitewater.

———◆———

Q. President John F. Kennedy was accused by his political foes of nepotism when he appointed what relative as attorney general?

A. His brother, Robert F. "Bobby" Kennedy.

———◆———

Q. Who was the first full-term president not to seek re-election?

A. James K. Polk.

Q. How old was Franklin Pierce when he became president?

A. Forty-eight.

Q. Who did President John F. Kennedy appoint in 1961 as the first director of the newly created Peace Corps?

A. His brother-in-law R. Sargent Shriver.

Q. By what title was President Harry S. Truman's policy on domestic issues known?

A. The Fair Deal.

Q. While taking the oath of office, what nineteenth-century president-elect substituted the term "affirm" in place of "swear"?

A. Franklin Pierce.

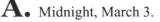

Q. Who was the first chief executive to receive a transcontinental telegram?

A. Abraham Lincoln.

Q. Since inauguration day fell on a Sunday, March 4, 1877, and fearing the possible maneuverings of political foes, President Ulysses S. Grant selected what time for the swearing in of President-elect Rutherford B. Hayes?

A. Midnight, March 3.

Q. Which chief executive was the first to hold White House press conferences on a regular basis?

A. Woodrow Wilson.

Q. Which president conducted a record 998 news conferences during his presidency?

A. Franklin D. Roosevelt.

———◆———

Q. What woman, brandishing an unloaded double-barreled pistol and stating that she was "sent by God Almighty to kill President Andrew Johnson," was taken into custody at the White House in 1869?

A. Annie O'Neil.

———◆———

Q. Which Union commander referred to President Abraham Lincoln as "nothing more than a well-meaning baboon"?

A. General George B. McClellan.

———◆———

Q. Sailing aboard the SS *George Washington,* who was the first chief executive to cross the Atlantic Ocean?

A. Woodrow Wilson.

———◆———

Q. How was the justice of the peace who first administered the presidential oath to President-elect Calvin Coolidge related to Coolidge?

A. He was his father.

———◆———

Q. Which president had a telegraph room installed in the White House?

A. Andrew Johnson.

———◆———

Q. Where did President Franklin D. Roosevelt meet with Allied leaders Winston Churchill and Joseph Stalin in February 1945?

A. Yalta, Ukraine.

Q. Gerald Ford extended a presidential pardon to what notorious World War II Axis radio personality?

A. Tokyo Rose (Iva Toguri D'Aquino).

Q. During Franklin Pierce's administration, what future president was appointed as minister to Great Britain?

A. James Buchanan.

Q. What vice president to Woodrow Wilson coined the phrase "What this country needs is a good five-cent cigar"?

A. Thomas Riley Marshall.

Q. Which president declared, "If you can't stand the heat, get out of the kitchen"?

A. Harry S. Truman.

Q. On January 13, 1966, who did President Lyndon B. Johnson appoint as the first African American to serve as a cabinet member?

A. Secretary of Housing and Urban Development Robert C. Weaver.

Q. What former Arkansas state employee filed a sexual harassment lawsuit against President Bill Clinton in 1994?

A. Paula Corbin Jones.

Q. President Ronald Reagan was known for dispensing what confectionery?

A. Jellybeans.

Q. Who was the first president to visit all fifty states?

A. Richard Nixon.

Q. By special permission of Congress, where was president Franklin Pierce's convalescing vice president, William Rufus de Vane King, allowed to take his oath of office?

A. Havana, Cuba.

Q. Who did President James Monroe send to Florida in 1817 to deal with the Seminole Indian uprising?

A. Major General Andrew Jackson.

Q. Who served as secretary of commerce in both Warren G. Harding's and Calvin Coolidge's administrations?

A. Herbert Hoover.

Q. Which president was noted for his "fireside chats" that were aired nationally on radio?

A. Franklin D. Roosevelt.

Q. United States air strikes were brought against what Libyan leader targeted by President Ronald Reagan as a sponsor of international terrorist activities?

A. Muammar al-Qaddafi.

Q. What did Calvin "Silent Cal" Coolidge say to the White House guest who told him that she had wagered she could get him to say more than two words to her?

A. "You lose."

Q. What ensuing scandal, sparked by a bungled burglary at the Democratic National Headquarters by agents of the Committee to Re-elect the President, led to President Richard Nixon's resignation?

A. Watergate.

———◆———

Q. Theodore Roosevelt pressed into service what 275-foot naval gunboat as a presidential vessel?

A. The *Mayflower.*

———◆———

Q. When the Prince of Wales and his large entourage visited the White House during James Buchanan's presidency, where did the president have to sleep in order to provide proper quarters for the many guests?

A. In a hallway.

———◆———

Q. In the spring of 1961, President John F. Kennedy and his administration orchestrated what failed paramilitary operation by CIA-trained-and-armed exiled Cubans?

A. Bay of Pigs invasion.

———◆———

Q. Who did President Ronald Reagan appoint in 1988 as the first Hispanic cabinet member and secretary of education?

A. Lauro F. Cavazos.

———◆———

Q. What presidential power did George Washington exercise for the first time in the nation's history in April 1792?

A. Veto.

———◆———

Q. Who was the first president to address the nation by radio?

A. Woodrow Wilson.

Q. Who was the first president to have his oath of office administered by a woman?

A. Lyndon B. Johnson (by Judge Sarah T. Hughes).

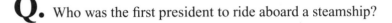

Q. How old was Theodore Roosevelt when he assumed the presidency following William McKinley's assassination?

A. Forty-two.

Q. Who was the first president to ride aboard a steamship?

A. James Monroe (the *Savannah,* 1819).

Q. How many U.S. Supreme Court appointments did President Ulysses S. Grant make during his two terms in office?

A. Four.

Q. In 1794 George Washington raised 15,000 troops to put down what rebellion by farmers in western Pennsylvania?

A. The Whiskey Rebellion.

Q. Whose presidential oath of office was administered on board Air Force One at Love Field in Dallas, Texas?

A. Lyndon B. Johnson (following John F. Kennedy's assassination).

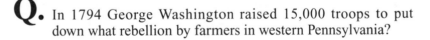

Q. Which president had only ninety dollars in cash when he left the presidency at age seventy?

A. Andrew Jackson.

Q. What was the length of George Washington's second inaugural speech?

A. 133 words.

Q. Who was the first president to be photographed while in office?

A. William Henry Harrison (1841).

Q. In April 1952 President Harry S. Truman ordered what major industrial facilities to be seized by the federal government?

A. Steel mills.

Q. In July 1963 President John F. Kennedy signed what treaty that ended atmospheric testing of nuclear weapons by the United States, the Soviet Union, and Great Britain?

A. Nuclear Test Ban Treaty.

Q. While serving as president, under whose name did Andrew Jackson register his racehorses in local Washington-area races to avoid possible bad press?

A. Andrew Donelson, Mrs. Jackson's nephew.

Q. In 1883 President Chester Arthur signed what piece of legislation creating the Civil Service System?

A. Pendleton Act.

Q. What 1,400-pound gift from a New York dairy farmer did President Andrew Jackson accept and share with the public on a "first come, first serve" basis?

A. Cheese.

Q. Who was appointed in 1800 by President John Adams to serve as governor of the Indiana Territory?

A. William Henry Harrison.

Q. What editor of the *New York Tribune* was Benjamin Harrison's running mate in Harrison's 1892 bid for re-election?

A. Whitelaw Reid.

Q. After the Civil War, who was the first president to be elected from the Deep South?

A. Jimmy Carter.

Q. Where in 1931-32 did Franklin D. Roosevelt have his "Little White House" built?

A. Warm Springs, Georgia.

Q. Which president was first to introduce into national politics the "spoils system" of rewarding supporters with government positions?

A. Andrew Jackson.

Q. What American, known as the "Grey-eyed Man of Destiny," did President Franklin Pierce acknowledge in 1856 as the newly elected president of Nicaragua?

A. William Walker.

Q. In an attempt to limit his caloric intake, President Richard Nixon often dined on what luncheon fare?

A. Cottage cheese and ketchup.

Q. Who did Franklin D. Roosevelt appoint in 1933 as the first woman cabinet member?

A. Frances Perkins (secretary of labor).

———◆———

Q. Early in his second term, President Ulysses S. Grant had to deal with what national financial crisis?

A. Panic of 1873.

———◆———

Q. In what event in October 1962 did President John F. Kennedy take an uncompromising stand that led the United States and the Soviet Union to the brink of nuclear war?

A. Cuban Missile Crisis.

———◆———

Q. To what imprisoned World War I protestor and leader of the Socialist Party did President Warren G. Harding grant a pardon in 1921?

A. Eugene V. Debs.

———◆———

Q. As governor of the Indiana Territory, William Henry Harrsion banned the sale of what commodity to the Indians within the territory?

A. Liquor.

———◆———

Q. During President Andrew Johnson's administration, what state was admitted to the Union?

A. Nebraska (1867).

———◆———

Q. Which president's legislative program was dubbed the Great Society?

A. Lyndon B. Johnson.

Q. In 1973 who became vice president in President Richard Nixon's administration when Spiro T. Agnew resigned the office under charges of accepting kickbacks and bribes and of income tax evasion?

A. Gerald Ford.

Q. In 1887 President Grover Cleveland signed what bill into law that created the nation's first federal regulatory agency?

A. Interstate Commerce Act (Interstate Commerce Commission).

Q. Although shot on July 2, 1881, President James A. Garfield did not succumb to blood poisoning and bronchopneumonia until when?

A. September 19, 1881.

Q. In what Philadelphia newspaper did George Washington publish his 6,000-word Farewell Address on September 19, 1796?

A. *American Daily Advertiser.*

Q. At what San Francisco hotel did President Warren G. Harding die on the evening of August 2, 1923?

A. Palace Hotel.

Q. Whose presidential inauguration was the first to be held in Washington, D.C.?

A. Thomas Jefferson's.

Q. Who did President Grover Cleveland appoint to his cabinet as the nation's first secretary of agriculture?

A. Norman J. Colman.

Q. Who served in President James K. Polk's cabinet as postmaster general and introduced the usage of postage stamps into the U.S. postal system?

A. Cave Johnson.

Q. What song did President Abraham Lincoln request to be played when he was called from the White House by throngs of Washingtonians excited over news of Robert E. Lee's surrender?

A. "Dixie."

Q. What distance did President Harry S. Truman briskly walk each morning for exercise?

A. Two miles.

Q. In 1957 President Dwight D. Eisenhower dispatched federal troops to what city to help curb violence due to desegregation?

A. Little Rock, Arkansas.

Q. Which president armed White House servants and stood down a mob of rioters who marched on, and broke out windows in, the White House?

A. John Tyler.

Q. Who was the first president to serve a nation consisting of 48 contiguous states?

A. William H. Taft (1912).

Q. In what type of automobile was President John F. Kennedy riding when he was shot in 1963?

A. A 1961 Lincoln Continental.

Q. What president and his cabinet helped fight a fire at the Library of Congress in 1851?

A. Millard Fillmore.

Q. What popular U.S. general did President Harry S. Truman relieve of his command in Korea in April 1951 for criticizing administration policies?

A. General Douglas MacArthur.

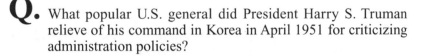

Q. In 1964 President Lyndon B. Johnson declared a "war" on what socioeconomic problem?

A. Poverty.

Q. What six states were admitted to the Union during Benjamin Harrison's administration?

A. North Dakota, South Dakota, Montana, Washington, Idaho, and Wyoming.

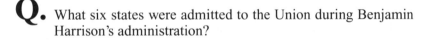

Q. Who was the first chief executive to appear on television?

A. Franklin D. Roosevelt (April 30, 1939).

Q. In 1924 Calvin Coolidge became the first president to order what make of automobile for the White House fleet?

A. Lincoln.

Q. On September 5, 1975, what disciple of mass murderer Charles Manson attempted to assassinate President Gerald Ford with a Colt .45 outside the Senator Hotel in Sacramento, California?

A. Lynette "Squeaky" Fromme.

Q. What term did Andrew Jackson apply to his group of unofficial advisers who met in the rear of the White House to discuss national issues?

A. "Kitchen Cabinet."

———◆———

Q. With what Caribbean island nation did President Dwight D. Eisenhower sever diplomatic relations in January 1961?

A. Cuba.

———◆———

Q. Whose arrival in San Francisco in 1880 marked the first time a president had visited the West Coast?

A. Rutherford B. Hayes's.

———◆———

Q. Who was the first president to be visited by a queen?

A. Andrew Johnson (Queen Emma of the Sandwich Islands).

———◆———

Q. President James A. Garfield was shot by his assassin in what public facility in Washington, D.C.?

A. Baltimore and Potomac railroad station.

———◆———

Q. What document was signed and issued by Abraham Lincoln on New Year's Day 1863 declaring the freedom of slaves in Confederate-controlled areas?

A. Emancipation Proclamation.

———◆———

Q. On President John Tyler's last full day in office he signed a bill admitting what state to the Union?

A. Florida.

Q. During whose administration did the first Christmas tree appear in the White House?

A. Benjamin Harrison's.

Q. How many electoral votes were cast against James Monroe in the election of 1820?

A. One (by elector William Plumer of New Hampshire in opposition to his state's popular vote).

Q. With whom did President Richard Nixon sign the SALT (Strategic Arms Limitation Talks) Agreement in May 1972?

A. Soviet leader Leonid Brezhnev.

Q. During President Ulysses S. Grant's two terms in office, how many persons served as attorney general in his cabinet?

A. Five.

Q. During his time in office, President Lyndon B. Johnson escalated the number of U.S. troops in Vietnam from the initial 3,500 sent to Danang in March 1965 to what peak 1968 figure?

A. 550,000.

Q. In 1934 President Franklin D. Roosevelt withdrew U.S. troops from what Caribbean nation?

A. Haiti.

Q. Whigs in the House of Representatives introduced what type of resolution on January 10, 1843, with regard to President John Tyler?

A. Impeachment.

Q. What noted piece of national health-care legislation did President Lyndon B. Johnson sign into law in Independence, Missouri, in 1965?

A. Medicare Act.

＋

Q. To what civil-war-torn African nation did President George Bush dispatch U.S. troops in December 1992 to assist in humanitarian relief efforts?

A. Somalia.

＋

Q. What was the name of President Franklin D. Roosevelt's massive federal economics and welfare program?

A. The New Deal.

＋

Q. In what year did President Rutherford B. Hayes withdraw the last federal troops from the South?

A. 1877.

＋

Q. Which chief executive inaugurated the interdenominational White House prayer breakfast?

A. Dwight D. Eisenhower.

＋

Q. President Ulysses S. Grant's first postmaster general, John A. J. Creswell, introduced what new stationery item into the U.S. postal system?

A. Penny postcard.

＋

Q. President Lyndon B. Johnson had to contend with North Korea's seizure of what U.S. intelligence ship in 1968?

A. USS *Pueblo.*

Q. Who was the first president to broadcast from the White House via television?

A. Harry S. Truman (1947).

———◆———

Q. Although he failed in his attempt, President Franklin Pierce wanted to annex what Caribbean island into the United States?

A. Cuba.

———◆———

Q. President William H. Taft dispatched U.S. Marines to what Latin American country to help its leaders put down rebel forces?

A. Nicaragua.

———◆———

Q. What vivacious actress drew much attention from the press for her sexy rendition of "Happy Birthday" to President John F. Kennedy?

A. Marilyn Monroe.

———◆———

Q. What Liberal Republican Party candidate, with a Democratic Party endorsement, was Ulysses S. Grant's strongest opponent in Grant's 1872 re-election bid?

A. Horace Greeley.

———◆———

Q. How many times was President James A. Garfield shot by his assassin?

A. Two (grazed right arm and lower back).

———◆———

Q. By what royal title did members of the Whig Party disparagingly refer to President Andrew Jackson?

A. "King Andrew I."

Q. In 1853 what president was arrested in Washington for accidentally running down an elderly lady with his horse?

A. Franklin Pierce.

Q. The poinsettia is named for what botanist and diplomat selected by President Martin Van Buren to serve as secretary of war?

A. Joel R. Poinsett.

Q. On January 17, 1991, President George Bush launched what military offensive against Iraq?

A. Operation Desert Storm.

Q. Who did President Martin Van Buren select in 1839 to secure a peace treaty in the border dispute between Maine and Canada known as the Aroostook War?

A. General Winfield Scott.

Q. On December 20, 1989, President George Bush sent U.S. troops into Panama to capture what drug-trafficking military leader?

A. General Manuel Antonio Noriega.

Q. What national policy with regard to European interference and expansion in the Americas was set forth by James Monroe in a speech to Congress on December 2, 1823?

A. The Monroe Doctrine.

Q. Although Samuel J. Tilden beat Rutherford B. Hayes by more than 250,000 popular votes, Hayes captured the presidency with how many more electoral votes than Tilden?

A. One.

Q. During President James A. Garfield's first week in office, he ordered the investigation of charges in what postal-related scandal?

A. Star Route Scandal.

Q. To what historical political figure did President Jimmy Carter restore U.S. citizenship in 1978?

A. Confederate President Jefferson Davis.

Q. What highly publicized overland mail service was established during President James Buchanan's administration?

A. Pony Express.

Q. What piece of legislation did President John Tyler approve in 1841 which allowed settlers to lay claim to 160 acres of federal land by constructing a cabin on the parcel?

A. Pre-emption Act.

Q. Gideon Welles, appointed by President Abraham Lincoln as secretary of the navy, introduced what type of military vessels into the nation's arsenal?

A. Ironclads.

Q. Who was the Republican Party's presidential candidate to oppose Franklin D. Roosevelt in 1944 and Harry S. Truman in 1948?

A. Thomas Dewey.

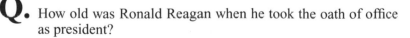

Q. How old was Ronald Reagan when he took the oath of office as president?

A. Sixty-nine.

Q. During President Andrew Johnson's administration, what large parcel of real estate was purchased from Russia by the United States for $1.2 million?

A. Alaska.

———◆———

Q. Who was the only member of John Tyler's cabinet not to resign in 1841 over the president's two-time veto of legislation to resurrect a national bank system?

A. Daniel Webster.

———◆———

Q. In the 1936 election, President Franklin D. Roosevelt's Republican opponent, Alfred M. Landon, carried how many states?

A. Two (Maine and Vermont).

———◆———

Q. Who was William McKinley's Democratic opponent in the presidential elections of 1896 and 1900?

A. William Jennings Bryan.

———◆———

Q. What three yachts were used by President Franklin D. Roosevelt?

A. *Sequoia, Potomac,* and *Williamsburg.*

———◆———

Q. What was the theme of a nightmare that Abraham Lincoln experienced and shared with friend Ward H. Lamon early in April 1865?

A. Presidential assassination.

———◆———

Q. After being sworn into office, President Harry S. Truman asked the press to do what for him?

A. Pray.

Q. Who was the first president to have his State of the Union address broadcast simultaneously on all major commercial television networks?

A. Lyndon B. Johnson (in 1967 on ABC, CBS, and NBC).

Q. In 1989 President George Bush signed into law a plan to bail out hundreds of what type of insolvent financial institutions?

A. Savings and loans.

Q. Who stated in his first presidential inaugural address, "The only thing we have to fear is fear itself"?

A. Franklin D. Roosevelt.

Q. President William McKinley called on Congress in April 1898 to authorize the military to take action against what European nation?

A. Spain.

Q. Who attempted to assassinate Franklin D. Roosevelt in Miami on February 15, 1933, and in doing so killed Chicago mayor Anton Cermak?

A. Giuseppe Zangara.

Q. Who was the first president to ride in a submarine?

A. Theodore Roosevelt.

Q. On board the USS *Augusta,* President Franklin D. Roosevelt's Scottish terrier, Fala, was present at the signing of what 1941 agreement between the United States and Great Britain?

A. The Atlantic Charter.

Q. Which of President Franklin Pierce's U.S. Supreme Court appointees later resigned his post to serve as assistant secretary of war in the Confederacy?

A. John A. Campbell.

———◆———

Q. What was the only rebel state to be completely exempted by President Abraham Lincoln from his Emancipation Proclamation?

A. Tennessee.

———◆———

Q. Who dedicated the Jefferson Memorial in Washington, D.C.?

A. President Franklin D. Roosevelt (1943).

———◆———

Q. In September 1974, who extended to former President Richard Nixon a "full, free, and absolute pardon" for any role he may have played in the Watergate scandal?

A. President Gerald Ford.

———◆———

Q. During John Tyler's term as president, what treaty was signed establishing the boundary between Maine and the Canadian province of New Brunswick?

A. Webster-Ashburton Treaty.

———◆———

Q. Upon assuming the presidency, who did President Gerald Ford nominate to fill the office of vice-president?

A. Nelson A. Rockefeller.

———◆———

Q. Who was the first chief executive to file an income tax return?

A. Warren G. Harding (1923).

Q. What 45,535-square-mile acquisition of land comprising the southern portions of present-day Arizona and New Mexico was made by the United States during Franklin Pierce's administration?

A. Gadsden Purchase (1853).

◆

Q. In 1938 President Franklin D. Roosevelt dedicated what bridge connecting the United States and Canada?

A. Thousand Islands Bridge.

◆

Q. What treaty did President Woodrow Wilson personally deliver to the U.S. Senate on July 10, 1919?

A. The Treaty of Versailles (which it rejected).

◆

Q. Who took a shot at President Gerald Ford with a .38 pistol on September 22, 1975, in San Francisco, California?

A. Sara Jane Moore.

◆

Q. In July 1995 President Bill Clinton announced the normalization of relations with what communist Southeast Asian nation?

A. Vietnam.

◆

Q. Who was the first U.S. president to address a joint session of the British Parliament?

A. Ronald Reagan (1982).

◆

Q. Who did President Millard Fillmore select to head an expedition to Japan and the Far East?

A. Commodore Matthew C. Perry.

Q. Which president shared with his cabinet that his recurring dream of being on board a ship that was rapidly moving "toward an indefinite shore" often preceded the arrival of good news?

A. Abraham Lincoln.

Q. During his terms in office, President Dwight D. Eisenhower signed what two statehood bills?

A. Alaska and Hawaii.

Q. President Lyndon B. Johnson signed what act that provided assistance with food purchases for the poor?

A. Food Stamp Act.

Q. On March 24, 1970, President Richard Nixon signed into law a measure which banned the advertising of what consumer product on radio and televison?

A. Cigarettes.

Q. Who referred to the presidency as "a splendid misery"?

A. Thomas Jefferson.

Q. What title was given to President Ronald Reagan's 1983 proposal for the development of earth/space technology to intercept and destroy enemy missiles?

A. "Star Wars."

Q. President Martin Van Buren fought with Congress over the ownership of what gift sent to the president of the United States from the sultan of Oman, Kabul al Said?

A. A pair of tiger cubs (Congress won).

Q. In 1794 President George Washington and the Congress authorized the creation of what branch of the U.S. Defense Department?

A. United States Navy.

———◆———

Q. On March 17, 1906, President Theodore Roosevelt used what term during a speech before the Gridiron Club in Washington, D.C., that became widely used in the press?

A. "Muckrake."

———◆———

Q. President Harry S. Truman announced the United States' development of what weapon of mass destruction during his January 7, 1953, State of the Union address?

A. Hydrogen bomb.

———◆———

Q. What memorial did President Warren G. Harding dedicate in Arlington National Cemetery on November 11, 1921?

A. Tomb of the Unknown Soldier.

———◆———

Q. Which president introduced the use of helicopters at the White House?

A. Dwight D. Eisenhower.

———◆———

Q. What program did President Lyndon B. Johnson promote that encouraged U.S. citizens to spend their tourist dollars in the United States?

A. "Discover America."

———◆———

Q. To whom did President Richard Nixon submit his letter of resignation?

A. Secretary of State Henry Kissinger.

Q. What did President Dwight D. Eisenhower have installed on the presidential airplane to help keep First Lady Mamie Eisenhower's mind off of flying?

A. A piano.

◆

Q. What influential black Democratic representative from New York helped Dwight D. Eisenhower garner 40 percent of the African-American vote in Eisenhower's 1956 presidential re-election bid?

A. Adam Clayton Powell, Jr.

◆

Q. The Department of Defense, Central Intelligence Agency, National Security Council, and the Joint Chiefs of Staff were all created under what act signed into law by President Harry S. Truman in July 1947?

A. National Security Act.

◆

Q. During a November 3, 1969, nationally televised address, President Richard Nixon called on what segment of America to support his administration's Vietnam War policy?

A. The "silent majority."

◆

Q. In 1879 President Rutherford B. Hayes signed legislation which allowed women lawyers the right to argue cases before what court?

A. U.S. Supreme Court.

◆

Q. To emphasize his right of succession to the presidency following President William Henry Harrison's death, John Tyler refused to open or acknowledge any mail addressed to him bearing what title?

A. "Acting President."

III

PRESIDENTIAL HOUSEHOLDS

Q. Who was the original first lady to enlist a Secret Service man for her own use?

A. Florence Harding.

Q. Which presidential family had a pet one-legged chicken?

A. The Theodore Roosevelt family.

Q. What candy bar is said to have been named for the popular infant daughter of President Grover Cleveland?

A. Baby Ruth.

Q. Which first lady, noted for her spending sprees, purchased 300 pairs of gloves during one four-month period?

A. Mary Todd Lincoln.

Q. Franklin D. Roosevelt was a seventh cousin once removed of what noted British leader?

A. Winston Churchill.

Q. What Greek shipping tycoon did former First Lady Jacqueline Kennedy marry in 1968?

A. Aristotle Onassis.

Q. Martha Washington was born in what Virginia county on June 21, 1731?

A. Kent County.

Q. Confederate President Jefferson Davis was the son-in-law of what U.S. president?

A. Zachary Taylor.

Q. Which first lady prided herself in tracing her ancestry to Pocahontas?

A. Edith Bolling Wilson.

Q. At age twenty-one, who was the youngest first lady?

A. Frances Cleveland.

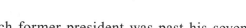

Q. Which former president was past his seventieth birthday when his fifteenth child was born?

A. John Tyler.

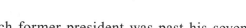

Q. For what reason was Andrew Jackson's pet parrot ejected from the room in which funeral ceremonies for Jackson were being held at the Hermitage?

A. Screaming obscenities at the mourners.

Q. Who was the first president to station police at the door of the White House?

A. Martin Van Buren.

Q. Which first lady was the first to occupy the Executive Mansion?

A. Abigail Adams.

Q. During John Tyler's presidency, what famous English author toured the White House and later commented about the visit in his *American Notes*?

A. Charles Dickens.

Q. Thomas Jefferson trained what favorite pet to sing along as Jefferson played his violin?

A. Dick the mockingbird.

Q. What language did President Herbert Hoover and his wife sometimes speak when they did not want White House visitors or staff members to know their conversation?

A. Chinese.

Q. Adorned with classical columns, what structural addition did Thomas Jefferson have made to the White House during his term in office?

A. A hen house.

Q. What twenty-four-year-old became John Tyler's second wife?

A. Julia Gardiner.

Q. Eleanor Roosevelt was such a somber and shy little girl that her mother gave her what nickname?

A. "Granny."

Q. At which first lady's insistence did Congress appropriate funds for indoor plumbing for the White House?

A. Abigail Fillmore.

Q. How old was Andrew Johnson when his first child, Martha, was born?

A. Nineteen.

Q. What former first lady's likeness appeared on the U.S. 1886 one-dollar silver certificate?

A. Martha Washington's.

Q. Where is Mary Todd Lincoln buried?

A. Oak Hill Cemetery, Springfield, Illinois.

Q. Eleanor Roosevelt made the news in 1939 when she served what dish to visiting King George VI and Queen Elizabeth?

A. Hot dogs.

Q. To how many other presidents was Franklin D. Roosevelt related by blood or marriage?

A. Eleven (John Adams, John Quincy Adams, Grant, William Henry Harrison, Benjamin Harrison, Madison, Theodore Roosevelt, Taft, Taylor, Van Buren, and Washington).

Q. Who was the first chief executive to have a personal valet?

A. Chester A. Arthur.

Q. Fearful of operating the switches to the first electric lights in the White House, which first family sometimes slept with all of the lights on?

A. The Benjamin Harrison family.

Q. When finding himself short of funds during poker games, President Warren G. Harding sometimes used what White House items with which to ante?

A. Pieces of fine china.

Q. William H. Taft hired George H. Robinson as the first person to fill what White House staff position?

A. Chauffeur.

Q. What executive couple had a pet canary named Johnny Ty?

A. John and Julia Tyler.

Q. In what Texas city were Lyndon B. Johnson and Claudia Alta "Lady Bird" Taylor married on November 17, 1934?

A. San Antonio.

Q. San Francisco astrologer Joan Quigley claimed she often gave advice by telephone to what first lady concerning matters of timing for travel and special political events?

A. Nancy Reagan.

Q. Who was the first presidential child to be born in the White House?

A. Esther Cleveland (born September 9, 1893).

Q. When Abraham Lincoln delivered his famous Gettysburg Address, what item was worn on his hat in memory of his son Willie who had died some nine months earlier?

A. A black crepe band.

Q. Who did Thelma Catherine "Pat" Ryan marry on June 21, 1940?

A. Richard Nixon.

Q. How many public appearances did First Lady Eliza McCardle Johnson make during her almost four years in the White House?

A. Two (a reception in 1866 and the president's birthday party in 1867).

Q. How many times did Rachel Robards marry Andrew Jackson?

A. Twice (1791 and 1794).

Q. Which first lady, during her emotionally devastating stay in the White House, often wrote letters to her dead son, Bennie?

A. Jane Pierce.

Q. Which president had security police bar African Americans from the grounds of the White House during his two terms in office?

A. Ulysses S. Grant.

Q. Who was first to become the bride of an incumbent president?

A. Frances Folsom (Cleveland).

Q. Which president became stuck in a White House bathtub?

A. William H. Taft, who weighed more than 300 pounds.

Q. Which president purchased a cow named Sukey to provide dairy products for the White House?

A. William Henry Harrison.

Q. During Mary Todd Lincoln's four-year stay at an exclusive girls' school in Lexington, Kentucky, what was the only language she and her fellow schoolmates were allowed to use in conversations?

A. French.

Q. Who is the only woman to have been a wife of a president and the mother of a president?

A. Abigail Adams.

Q. Which president had his son Abraham work as his White House secretary?

A. Martin Van Buren.

Q. When Caroline Harrison moved into the White House, she found the attic to be heavily infested with what manner of vermin?

A. Rats.

Q. Who was the first president to lie in state in the East Room of the White House?

A. William Henry Harrison.

Q. Which first lady was known for often wearing a forehead jewel?

A. Julia Tyler.

Q. Although electricity had been used in the White House for several years, Frances Cleveland insisted on what type of lighting in the Red Room?

A. A single kerosene oil lamp.

Q. By what nickname was Lucretia Garfield known to her husband and close friends?

A. "Crete."

Q. Who was best man at the 1975 wedding of Bill Clinton and Hillary Rodham?

A. Roger Clinton (Bill Clinton's half-brother).

Q. What communication device did President Rutherford B. Hayes have installed in the White House for the first time in 1879?

A. Telephone.

Q. First Lady "Pat" Nixon was given her nickname by her parents because she was born on the eve of what holiday?

A. Saint Patrick's Day.

Q. Under whose administration was money appropriated to establish the first White House entertainment fund for official receptions and state dinners?

A. Warren G. Harding's.

Q. John Quincy and Louisa Adams raised what insects at the White House?

A. Silkworms.

Q. By lineage, how was Eleanor Roosevelt related to Franklin D. Roosevelt?

A. Fifth cousin once removed.

Q. Often referred to in the media as "Miss Lillian," which president's mother became a Peace Corps volunteer at age 68?

A. Lillian Carter (Jimmy Carter's mother).

Q. Pregnant at age nineteen, who did the future First Lady Florence Harding first marry in 1880?

A. Henry "Pete" DeWolfe.

Q. In 1983 Lady Bird Johnson founded what organization?

A. National Wildflower Research Center.

Q. Due to her White House ban on serving alcoholic beverages at state events, First Lady Lucy Hayes was given what nickname?

A. "Lemonade Lucy."

Q. During the American Revolution, Abigail Adams donated a portion of what personal collection to minutemen to melt down into bullets?

A. Spoon collection.

———◆———

Q. What was the relationship of Benjamin Harrison to William Henry Harrison?

A. Grandson.

———◆———

Q. What former first lady, who overcame her personal abuse of alcohol and pain-killing drugs, established a chemical dependency recovery center?

A. Betty Ford (the Betty Ford Center).

———◆———

Q. Who was the first president to use stationery which read "The White House" rather than "The Executive Mansion"?

A. Theodore Roosevelt.

———◆———

Q. Who was the first incumbent first lady to travel to Africa?

A. Pat Nixon (1972).

———◆———

Q. Because of the lack of outside clotheslines, what area of the White House did Abigail Adams use for the drying of laundry?

A. The East Room.

———◆———

Q. Both James A. Garfield and his wife, Lucretia, were natives of what Ohio county?

A. Cuyahoga.

Q. In April 1964, what did President Lyndon B. Johnson do that made national headlines and garnered the ire of dog lovers?

A. Picked up his beagle hounds by their ears.

Q. What item did First Lady Grace Coolidge make as a permanent item for the furnishing of the White House?

A. A crocheted bedspread.

Q. How many boys did Andrew and Rachel Jackson raise either by adoption or as their wards?

A. Four (Andrew Jackson, Jr., John Donelson, Andrew Jackson Donelson, and Andrew Jackson Hutchings).

Q. What first lady was the first to call publicly for the appointment of a woman to the U.S. Supreme Court?

A. Pat Nixon.

Q. To celebrate Julia Gardiner's acceptance of President John Tyler's proposal of marriage, Tyler imported a pair of what breed of dogs to occupy the White House?

A. Italian wolfhounds.

Q. Who was the only president who was also the son of a president?

A. John Quincy Adams.

Q. In 1975 First Lady Betty Ford made a cameo appearance on what television comedy show?

A. *The Mary Tyler Moore Show.*

Q. Which first lady was cross-eyed?

A. Julia Grant.

Q. Who was the first American woman to be presented at the royal court in England?

A. Abigail Adams.

Q. Who chose the site for the Executive Mansion?

A. George Washington.

Q. With her departure from the White House in 1909, Edith Kermit Roosevelt had the remains of her dead pets exhumed from one of the Executive Mansion's gardens and moved to what family estate?

A. Sagamore Hill (at Oyster Bay, New York).

Q. What were the names of Martha Washington's two children by her first husband?

A. John "Jackie" Parke Custis and Martha "Patsy" Parke Custis.

Q. Laddie Boy, Warren G. Harding's most famous pet, was what breed of dog?

A. Airedale.

Q. Which former first lady had a grove in the Redwood National Park dedicated in her name in 1969?

A. Lady Bird Johnson.

Q. Who was the only bachelor president to occupy the White House?

A. James Buchanan.

Q. Which first lady was noted in Washington for her "little red book" in which she listed her and her husband's enemies?

A. Florence Harding.

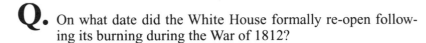

Q. On what date did the White House formally re-open following its burning during the War of 1812?

A. New Year's Day, 1818.

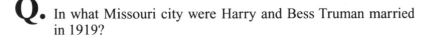

Q. In what Missouri city were Harry and Bess Truman married in 1919?

A. Independence.

Q. By what childhood nickname did George Washington call Martha Washington?

A. "Patsy."

Q. Following the burning of the White House by British troops, what became James and Dolley Madison's residence?

A. The Octagon House.

Q. As a teenager, Eleanor Roosevelt attended what girls' finishing school near London, England, for three years?

A. Allenswood.

Q. Following the burning of Washington, D.C., by the British, who persuaded President James Madison not to move the nation's capital back to Philadelphia?

A. Dolley Madison.

Q. When Martha Dandridge Custis married George Washington in 1759, what was the name of her plantation home?

A. White House.

Q. By what name was Franklin D. Roosevelt's Scottish terrier, Fala (Murry of Fala Hill), first known?

A. Big Boy.

Q. Who did James Buchanan appoint as his official hostess and overseer of White House functions?

A. Harriet Lane (Buchanan's niece).

Q. Where was the summer home of President Grover Cleveland and family?

A. Buzzard's Bay, Cape Cod, Massachusetts.

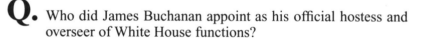

Q. During whose administration was the White House, for the first time, thoroughly photographed?

A. Benjamin Harrison's.

Q. Which daughter of Ronald Reagan told reporters in 1984 that both she and her husband had seen the ghost of Abraham Lincoln in the White House?

A. Maureen Reagan (husband Dennis Revell).

Q. Who first served ice cream at the White House?

A. Dolley Madison.

———◆———

Q. William Henry Harrison's father was a signer of what famous document?

A. Declaration of Independence.

———◆———

Q. In her 1891 book, *Was Abraham Lincoln a Spiritualist?*, what medium claimed to have conducted several séances in the White House during the Lincoln administration?

A. Nettie Colburn.

———◆———

Q. Where was Hillary Rodham Clinton born (October 26, 1947)?

A. Chicago, Illinois.

———◆———

Q. What former president married his wife's former nurse, four years after his wife's death?

A. Benjamin Harrison.

———◆———

Q. Which early first lady was terrified of thunderstorms?

A. Abigail Adams.

———◆———

Q. What was the name of the golden retriever that often shared the Oval Office with President Gerald Ford?

A. Liberty.

Q. Who was John F. Kennedy's best man at his wedding?

A. Robert F. "Bobby" Kennedy.

———◆———

Q. Who was the first wife of a president to attend her husband's inauguration?

A. Dolley Madison.

———◆———

Q. Who has been the only foreign-born first lady?

A. Louisa Adams (born London, England, 1775).

———◆———

Q. During whose administration was the north portico constructed on the White House?

A. Andrew Jackson's.

———◆———

Q. Which first lady's wedding ring was purchased at Sears and Roebuck for $2.50?

A. Lady Bird Johnson.

———◆———

Q. Which son of President Ronald Reagan was a member of the Joffrey Ballet?

A. Ronald Prescott Reagan.

———◆———

Q. Two years prior to marrying John F. Kennedy, Jacqueline Bouvier earned a degree in what subject from George Washington University?

A. Art history.

Q. What was Zachary Taylor's relationship to Robert E. Lee?

A. Fourth cousin once removed.

Q. On what date did Abraham Lincoln marry Mary Todd?

A. November 4, 1842.

Q. What was First Lady Letitia Tyler's favorite hobby?

A. Knitting.

Q. Who was the first child of a presidential family to appear in the buff in *Playboy* magazine?

A. Patti (Reagan) Davis.

Q. Which presidential canine, along with her pups, made the cover of *Life* magazine?

A. The Bushes' Millie.

Q. What age was former First Lady Bess Truman when she died of congestive heart failure in 1982?

A. Ninety-seven.

Q. What type of lighting was installed in the White House during the James K. Polk administration?

A. Gas lights.

Q. What religious leader sent a blessing to be read at the wedding of John F. Kennedy and Jacqueline Bouvier?

A. Pope Pius XII.

Q. What first lady penned a play in 1826 entitled *Suspicion*?

A. Louisa Adams.

Q. Who was the first president to marry while in office?

A. John Tyler.

Q. An accident with what type of vehicle brought about the demise of President Rutherford B. Hayes's greyhound, Grim?

A. A train.

Q. In the May 1995 issue of *Outlaw Biker* magazine, who was selected as "First Lady of the Century"?

A. Barbara Bush.

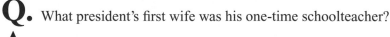

Q. What president's first wife was his one-time schoolteacher?

A. Millard Fillmore's.

Q. Which first lady was the first to serve as her husband's official secretary while in the White House?

A. Sarah Childress Polk.

Q. What was First Lady Rosalynn Carter's Secret Service code name?

A. "Dancer."

Q. On March 19, 1813, who became John Tyler's first wife?

A. Letitia Christian.

Q. Who was the only son of Franklin D. Roosevelt to become a member of the Republican Party?

A. John Aspinwall Roosevelt.

Q. What was the favorite food of the Theodore Roosevelt family's blue macaw, Eli Yale?

A. Coffee grounds.

Q. What Maryland native did twenty-five-year-old Zachary Taylor marry on June 21, 1810?

A. Margaret "Peggy" Mackall Smith.

Q. In 1965 Lady Bird Johnson helped win passsage of what legislation that limited the visual clutter of billboards and junkyards along major highways?

A. Highway Beautification Act.

Q. Who did William Henry Harrison marry on November 25, 1795?

A. Anna Symmes.

Q. What did Ulysses S. Grant call his wife, Julia?

A. "Mrs. G."

Q. Jane Pierce suffered from what disease for much of her adult life?

A. Tuberculosis.

Q. Which first lady was the first to conduct a televised tour of the White House?

A. Jacqueline Kennedy (1962).

Q. Which first lady was born in 1790 at Cedar Grove plantation in New Kent County, Virginia.

A. Letitia Christian Tyler.

Q. To whom was Rachel Jackson first married?

A. Captain Lewis Robards.

Q. During his term in office, which president reduced the White House fleet of 131 limousines to 20?

A. Lyndon B. Johnson.

Q. Who did Caroline Lavinia Scott marry on October 20, 1853?

A. Benjamin Harrison.

Q. Where did Martha Washington die on May 22, 1802?

A. Mount Vernon, Virginia.

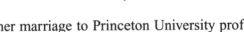

Q. In 1985 what became the Reagans' first White House pet?

A. Lucky, a sheepdog.

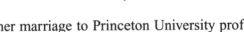

Q. To what wealthy Virginia planter was Martha Washington first married?

A. Daniel Parke Custis.

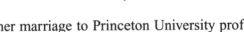

Q. What presidential family's Welsh terrier, named Charlie, was a nephew to the dog that played the role of Asta in the classic movie *The Thin Man*?

A. The Kennedys.

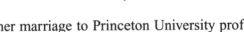

Q. With her marriage to Princeton University professor Thomas Preston, Jr., who became the first widowed former first lady to remarry?

A. Frances Cleveland.

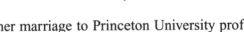

Q. What did former First Lady Edith Bolling Wilson carry with her to John F. Kennedy's inauguration to help dispel the cold?

A. A flask of bourbon.

Q. Which chief executive's mother was a practicing physician?

A. Warren G. Harding's (Phoebe Harding).

Q. On what date did Theodore Roosevelt's mother and his first wife, Alice, both die in the same house?

A. February 14, 1884.

Q. To whom did Ann Coleman of Lancaster, Pennsylvania, become engaged in 1819?

A. James Buchanan.

Q. By what pet name did Frances Cleveland call Grover Cleveland?

A. "Uncle Cleve."

Q. What brought about the demise of both of John Tyler's wives?

A. Stroke.

Q. Who did Louise Catherine Johnson marry on July 26, 1797?

A. John Quincy Adams.

Q. Which first lady was born in the month of October, married in October, and died in October?

A. Caroline Harrison.

Q. Which first lady had been a model with the Powers Modeling Agency in New York?

A. Betty Ford.

Q. What was Caroline Harrison's nickname?

A. "Carrie."

Q. What promise did Grover Cleveland exclude from the traditional marriage vows at his and Frances Folsom's White House wedding?

A. To obey.

Q. What was First Lady Julia Grant's favorite flower?

A. Cape jasmine.

Q. What actor served as best man at Ronald and Nancy Reagan's wedding?

A. William Holden.

Q. James Monroe owned a pair of sheepdogs that were a gift from what noted Frenchman?

A. The marquis de Lafayette.

Q. Which first lady was given the nickname "the Steel Magnolia?"

A. Rosalynn Carter.

Q. What was the reaction of Mrs. Franklin Pierce upon being told that her husband had received the Democratic Party's nomination to run for the presidency in the 1852 election?

A. She fainted.

Q. During the Civil War, which president's mother, along with her Confederate-sympathizing family, was incarcerated in a Federal detention camp?

A. Harry S. Truman's.

Q. Of which two presidents' wives are there no known actual portraits?

A. Martha Jefferson and Margaret Taylor.

Q. Which first lady received much media attention when she ordered 220 place settings of red and gold Lenox china for the White House at a cost of $209,508?

A. Nancy Reagan.

Q. Which first lady had a brother and three half-brothers who fought for the Confederacy during the Civil War?

A. Mary Todd Lincoln.

Q. Which first lady referred to the White House as "the Great White Jail"?

A. Bess Truman.

Q. What was Florence Harding's maiden name?

A. Florence "Flossie" Mabel Kling.

Q. What long-time pet of James and Dolley Madison is said to have outlived both the president and the first lady?

A. A parrot.

Q. On what day of the week did Sarah Childress Polk refuse to allow visitors at the White House?

A. Sunday.

Q. What series of motion pictures, starring Bing Crosby, Bob Hope, and Dorothy Lamour, did Bess Truman say were her favorite movies?

A. The "Road" movies.

Q. Including Jacqueline Kennedy, how many first ladies, either former or future, attended John F. Kennedy's inauguration?

A. Eight.

Q. Four generations of the Adams family lived in what Quincy, Massachusetts, house purchased by John Adams in 1787?

A. Peacefield.

Q. Which first lady was an extra in the motion pictures *Ben Hur* and *The Great Ziegfeld*?

A. Pat Nixon (Pat Ryan).

Q. In the 1890s, which son of Ulysses S. Grant helped develop Tijuana, Mexico, as a gambling resort?

A. Jesse Root Grant.

Q. Originally given to the White House for a Christmas dinner, what animal was adopted by the Lincolns and named Jack?

A. A turkey.

Q. In 1851 forty-year-old Margaret Sylvester declined a marriage proposal from what sixty-eight-year-old suitor?

A. Martin Van Buren.

Q. In 1806 who became the first child born in the White House?

A. James Madison Randolph (President Thomas Jefferson's grandson).

Q. What actress became Ronald Reagan's second wife on March 4, 1952?

A. Nancy Davis (born Anne Frances Robbins).

Q. John Tyler was a great-uncle of which president?

A. Harry S. Truman.

Q. What two beagles, which Lyndon B. Johnson brought to the White House when he assumed the presidency, made the cover of the June 19, 1964, issue of *Life* magazine?

A. Him and Her.

Q. Who was the first girl to be born in the Executive Mansion?

A. Letitia Tyler (President John Tyler's granddaughter).

Q. Where was Herbert Hoover when he cabled his marriage proposal to Lou Henry in California?

A. Australia.

Q. Which first lady conducted china-painting classes at the White House?

A. Caroline Harrison.

Q. What security code name was assigned to Eleanor Roosevelt during World War II?

A. "Rover."

Q. What bovine livestock did Andrew Johnson bring to the White House upon assuming the role of president?

A. Two Jersey cows.

Q. In 1984 what book by former First Lady Rosalynn Carter became a bestseller?

A. *First Lady from Plains.*

Q. Mrs. Caroline Carmichael McIntosh became which president's second wife on February 10, 1858?

A. Millard Fillmore's.

Q. President Bill Clinton's daughter, Chelsea Victoria, was named after what Joni Mitchell musical composition?

A. "Chelsea Morning."

Q. While in boarding school, Bess Truman participated in, and won, what track and field event?

A. Shot put.

Q. Following her marriage to Martin Van Buren's son Abraham in 1838, what South Carolina belle became the White House hostess?

A. Angelica Singleton Van Buren.

Q. Which president was known for feeding mice at the White House?

A. Andrew Johnson.

Q. Mrs. Jaffray, William H. Taft's White House housekeeper, refused to ride in what mode of transportation?

A. Automobile.

Q. Who served as the official Executive Mansion hostess during Thomas Jefferson's administration?

A. Dolley Madison.

Q. What former first lady lost her two front teeth in a 1946 automobile accident?

A. Eleanor Roosevelt.

Q. Caroline Kennedy's pony, Macaroni, which received thousands of fan letters from children across the nation, was a gift from what prominent politician?

A. Lyndon B. Johnson.

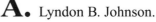

Q. For what movie did Ronald Reagan's first wife, Jane Wyman, win an Oscar (for best actress in 1948)?

A. *Johnny Belinda.*

Q. How was Ulysses S. Grant related to Grover Cleveland?

A. Sixth cousin once removed.

———◆———

Q. Although Thomas Jefferson compiled a voluminous personal diary, what does the single one-sentence entry about his mother address?

A. Date and time of her death.

———◆———

Q. Where were George and Barbara Bush married in 1945?

A. Rye, New York.

———◆———

Q. Zachary Taylor's mother's hands were permanently disfigured as the result of an accident while she was casting what items?

A. Bullets.

———◆———

Q. What Irish-born architect's design was selected as the original design for the Executive Mansion in Washington?

A. James Hoban's.

———◆———

Q. On April 3, 1800, Martha Washington became the first former first lady to receive what perk from the federal government?

A. Franking privileges (free postage).

———◆———

Q. Former First Lady Eleanor Roosevelt declined an offer to be seated on the main platform at John F. Kennedy's inauguration because of her great dislike for which Kennedy family member?

A. Joseph Kennedy (the president's father).

Q. Which presidential son was appointed secretary of the interior in 1907 by President Theodore Roosevelt?

A. James Rudolph Garfield.

Q. In what tobacco product did First Lady Dolley Madison indulge?

A. Snuff.

Q. Due to his mother's failing health, which president paid for the installation of a special telegraph line between the White House and his mother's home in Canton, Ohio?

A. William McKinley.

Q. Who was the first chief executive to have been divorced?

A. Ronald Reagan.

Q. Which former first lady was committed by her son for a three-month stay at a mental institution in Batavia, Illinois?

A. Mary Todd Lincoln.

Q. Ronald Reagan proposed to his first wife, Jane Wyman, on the set of what motion picture?

A. *Brother Rat.*

Q. How long before the 1892 election, in which Benjamin Harrison sought a second term, did Caroline Harrison die?

A. Two weeks.

Q. Which first lady oversaw the purchase of the White House's first cooking stove?

A. Abigail Fillmore.

Q. Which former first lady has been pictured on a U.S. postal card?

A. Martha Washington.

Q. In 1911 which former first lady was comatose for nine days after being thrown from a horse?

A. Helen Taft.

Q. What actress did Ronald Reagan marry on January 26, 1940?

A. Jane Wyman (Sarah Jane Fulks).

Q. When President Theodore Roosevelt's son Archie was sick, what did his sons Kermit and Quentin bring up in the White House elevator to cheer up Archie?

A. Archie's pony, Algonquin.

Q. In the 1980s, what son of Gerald Ford was a regular actor on the televison soap opera *The Young and the Restless*?

A. Steven Ford.

Q. Although later recovered and re-interred, the body of which president's father was exhumed by grave robbers and sold to the Ohio Medical College in Cincinnati for use as a training cadaver?

A. Benjamin Harrison's (John Scott Harrison).

Q. First Lady Lucy Hayes used what term to refer to her menagerie of White House pets?

A. Her "Noah's collection."

Q. What was First Lady Edith Bolling Wilson's favorite entrée?

A. Lobster Newburg.

Q. Franklin Pierce's father, Benjamin Pierce, was governor of what state for two terms?

A. New Hampshire.

Q. In 1881 Lucretia Garfield contracted what illness?

A. Malaria.

Q. In 1991 First Lady Barbara Bush suffered what injury while sledding at Camp David?

A. Broken leg.

Q. Who was the only man to be both the son and the father of a president?

A. John Scott Harrison.

Q. While waiting in a Paris prison for the guillotine, which had already dispatched her mother and grandmother, the marquis de Lafayette's wife, Adrienne, was freed following the visit of what future first lady?

A. Elizabeth Monroe.

Q. What was the last motion picture in which Nancy Reagan appeared?

A. *Crash Landing* (1958).

Q. Which president was the first not to outlive his father?

A. Warren G. Harding.

Q. During whose administration was Rebecca the raccoon a resident of the White House?

A. Calvin Coolidge.

Q. What was Thomas Jefferson's ancestral background?

A. Welsh.

Q. Where were John F. and Jacqueline Kennedy married on September 12, 1953?

A. Newport, Rhode Island.

Q. The addition of what item to the exterior of the White House during Harry S. Truman's administration required a new engraving to be made of the Executive Mansion for use on the back of twenty-dollar bills?

A. A new porch.

Q. In 1919 future First Lady Lou Hoover was decorated by what European head of state in honor of her relief work during World War I?

A. Albert, king of Belgium.

Q. What first lady was the first to ride in the same carriage back to the White House with the newly sworn-in president?

A. Helen Taft.

Q. First Lady Lucy Hayes was the first person in the United States to own what breed of cat?

A. Siamese.

Q. Who served as the first president-general of the Daughters of the American Revolution?

A. Caroline Harrison.

Q. Who did Elizabeth "Betty" Anne Bloomer marry in Grand Rapids, Michigan, on October 15, 1948?

A. Gerald Ford.

Q. Who did Jacqueline Kennedy admit to be her favorite first lady?

A. Bess Truman.

Q. During whose administration was central heat installed in the Executive Mansion?

A. Franklin Pierce (1853).

Q. What internationally famous designer did President Chester Arthur enlist to redecorate and furnish the White House?

A. Louis Comfort Tiffany.

Q. Which president had a dog named Veto?

A. James A. Garfield.

Q. Who had the annual Easter egg roll relocated from the Capitol grounds to the White House lawn?

A. Lucy Hayes.

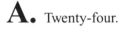

Q. President Theodore Roosevelt reprimanded which of his young sons for throwing spitballs at a White House portrait of Andrew Jackson?

A. Quentin Roosevelt.

Q. How old was Jacqueline Bouvier when she married thirty-six-year-old John F. Kennedy in 1953?

A. Twenty-four.

Q. President William H. Taft's first White House cow, Mooly Wooly, was replaced by what Holstein which grazed on the lawn of the Executive Mansion?

A. Pauline Wayne.

Q. Barbara Bush's father, Marvin Pierce, was the publisher of what two national magazines?

A. *McCall's* and *Redbook.*

Q. What two sons of presidents have received the Congressional Medal of Honor?

A. James Webb Hayes (Spanish-American War) and Theodore Roosevelt, Jr. (World War II).

Q. By what nickname did Grover Cleveland call his wife Frances?

A. "Frank."

Q. Prior to becoming first lady, Edith Bolling Galt (Wilson) was the first woman in Washington, D.C., to own what type of transportation?

A. An electric car.

Q. What former first lady was married to furniture salesman William C. Warren from 1942 until their divorce in 1947?

A. Betty Ford.

Q. Which son of Theodore Roosevelt was killed in a dogfight over France in 1918?

A. Quentin Roosevelt.

Q. Where were Herbert Hoover and Lou Henry married on February 10, 1899?

A. Monterey, California.

Q. Which first lady was born in Boone, Iowa, on November 14, 1896?

A. Mamie Eisenhower.

Q. What cud-chewing pets belonging to Tad Lincoln often had the run of the White House?

A. A pair of goats, Nanny and Nanko.

Q. What son of a president died at age sixteen as the result of infection from a blister incurred on his toe during a tennis game?

A. Calvin Coolidge, Jr.

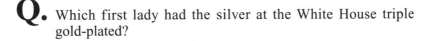

Q. How many children did James K. and Sarah Polk have?

A. None.

Q. Which first lady had the silver at the White House triple gold-plated?

A. Florence Harding.

Q. Who was the first president to have both parents alive upon assuming the presidency?

A. Ulysses S. Grant.

Q. What actress in her 1969 autobiography claimed to be a descendant of President Zachary Taylor?

A. Lillian Gish.

Q. A Siamese cat named Chan accompanied what presidential family to the White House?

A. The Fords.

Q. Bone marrow tuberculosis claimed the life of what former first lady in New York City on November 7, 1962?

A. Eleanor Roosevelt.

Q. Prior to serving as first lady, Lou Hoover served as president of what organization for girls?

A. Girl Scouts of America.

Q. John Quincy and Louisa Adams's youngest son, Charles Francis Adams, served as minister to what nation during the Civil War?

A. Great Britain.

Q. According to President Lyndon B. Johnson, his dog Yuki barked with what type of accent?

A. Texan.

Q. Who did Mamie Geneva Doud marry on July 1, 1916?

A. Dwight D. Eisenhower.

Q. First Lady Florence Harding was especially fond of what brand of chewing gum?

A. Beeman's pepsin chewing gum.

Q. When Lou Hoover enrolled at Stanford University in 1894, she was the only female student majoring in what subject?

A. Geology.

Q. Dancing, card playing, and alcoholic beverages were banned from the White House by what nineteenth-century first lady with strong Moravian ethics?

A. Sarah Childress Polk.

Q. What son of Abraham and Mary Todd Lincoln served as president of the railroad car manufacturing firm, the Pullman Company, from 1897 to 1911?

A. Robert Todd Lincoln.

Q. Which son of Theodore Roosevelt served as governor of Puerto Rico from 1929 to 1932 and governor-general of the Philippines in 1932 and 1933?

A. Theodore Roosevelt, Jr.

Q. How was Martin Van Buren related to Theodore Roosevelt?

A. Third cousin twice removed.

Q. What was the name of William Henry Harrison's widowed daughter-in-law who served as White House hostess during his brief term in office?

A. Jane Irwin Harrison.

Q. What Siamese cat accompanied the Carters to the White House?

A. Misty Malarky Ying Yang.

Q. In which room of the White House did the wedding of Grover Cleveland and Frances Folsom take place?

A. Blue Room.

Q. What large carnivores were brought back by Lewis and Clark from their western expedition, presented to Thomas Jefferson, and housed in cages on the White House grounds?

A. Grizzly bears.

Q. What was the name of Andrew Jackson's favorite pet parrot?

A. Poll.

Q. Which of Abraham Lincoln's sons was born with a cleft palate?

A. Thomas "Tad."

Q. What was the title of Nancy Reagan's autobiography published in 1989?

A. *My Turn.*

Q. What childhood sweetheart did Martin Van Buren marry on February 21, 1807?

A. Hannah Hoes.

Q. Which first lady's maiden name was the same as her name after she married?

A. Eleanor Roosevelt's.

Q. How old was Martha Dandridge Custis when she married George Washington on January 6, 1759?

A. Twenty-seven.

Q. What took the life of Hannah Van Buren seventeen years before her husband, Martin, was elected president of the United States?

A. Tuberculosis.

Q. What brother to Jimmy Carter became the namesake of a brand of beer?

A. Billy Carter (Billy Beer).

Q. What was the name of William McKinley's pet parrot that enjoyed chattering phrases at White House guests?

A. Washington Post.

Q. Martin Van Buren always called his wife, Hannah, by what Dutch form of her name?

A. Jannetje.

Q. Although not related, how did Sarah Childress Polk fondly refer to Andrew Jackson?

A. "Uncle Andrew."

Q. What was the name of Abraham Lincoln's first son, born in 1843?

A. Robert Todd.

Q. What best-selling book did Nan Britton publish in 1927 revealing details of her illicit affair with Warren G. Harding and information about their love child?

A. *The President's Daughter.*

Q. What was Eleanor Roosevelt's first name?

A. Anna.

Q. Martin and Hannah Van Buren had how many sons?

A. Four (Abraham, John, Martin, Jr., and Smith Thompson).

Q. William Henry Harrison's daughter-in-law Clarissa was the daughter of what famous explorer of the western United States?

A. Zebulon Pike.

Q. What was the name of President Theodore Roosevelt's six-toed cat?

A. Slippers.

Q. Which presidential son was dismisssed from his Andrew Jackson-appointed job with the Vincennes Land Office in Indiana after being charged with embezzling some $12,000 in agency funds?

A. John Cleves Symmes Harrison (son of William Henry Harrison).

Q. Noted colonial Virginia landholder James Taylor was the great-grandfather of which two U.S. presidents?

A. James Madison and Zachary Taylor.

Q. Prior to becoming first lady, who served for fourteen years as the circulation manager at the *Marion Star* in Marion, Ohio?

A. Florence Harding.

Q. James K. Polk was a great-great-grandnephew of what noted sixteenth-century Scottish religious leader?

A. John Knox.

Q. Who was the first former first lady to receive a pension for being a president's widow?

A. Anna Symmes Harrison.

Q. Which of Zachary Taylor's children served as commander of Confederate forces west of the Mississippi River in 1864 and 1865?

A. Lieutenant General Richard "Dick" Taylor.

Q. James Buchanan was of what ancestry?

A. Scotch-Irish.

Q. What first lady caught a cold at Franklin Pierce's outdoor inaugural ceremony, which evolved into pneumonia, resulting in her death a few weeks later?

A. Abigail Fillmore.

Q. Who did Barbara Bush reveal as being "the first man I ever kissed"?

A. George Bush.

Q. A total of 19,134 pennies donated by newsboys were melted down and molded into a statue of which president's dog?

A. Warren G. Harding's (Laddie Boy).

Q. Composer Stephen C. Foster's sister Ann Eliza was a sister-in-law to which president?

A. James Buchanan.

Q. Which president's term saw two first ladies?

A. John Tyler (Letitia Christian Tyler and Julia Gardiner Tyler).

Q. Which presidential son helped found the company that evolved into Union Carbide?

A. James Webb Hayes (also known as Webb Cook, son of Rutherford and Lucy Hayes).

Q. What type of footwear did First Lady Lou Hoover never wear?

A. High heels.

Q. Who was the first president to have his mother present at his inauguration?

A. James A. Garfield (mother, Eliza Ballou Garfield).

Q. In her later years, former First Lady Julia Grant resided in New York City and developed a close friendship with what former political foe?

A. Varina Davis (wife of Jefferson Davis, president of the Confederacy).

Q. When John Tyler was elected president, Letitia Tyler was suffering from the effects of what malady?

A. Paralytic stroke.

Q. For what final reason did the Eisenhowers exile their Weimaraner named Heidi from the White House to their Gettysburg, Pennsylvania, farm?

A. Urinating on the new carpet.

Q. What was the occasion of Letitia Tyler's only public appearance at the White House?

A. Her daughter Elizabeth's wedding.

———◆———

Q. What presidential daughter was arrested in 1985 in South Africa for illegally protesting apartheid?

A. Amy Carter (daughter of Jimmy and Rosalynn Carter).

———◆———

Q. What ailment took the life of Chester A. Arthur's wife, Ellen "Nell," in 1880?

A. Pneumonia.

———◆———

Q. During Harry S. Truman's administration, what noted seer's cat on several occasions wandered uninvited into the White House?

A. Jeane Dixon's.

———◆———

Q. What sister of Jimmy Carter was an evangelist and faith healer?

A. Ruth Carter Stapleton.

———◆———

Q. What first lady referred to the White House as being "a castle of a house"?

A. Abigail Adams.

———◆———

Q. What agency was enlisted to trap squirrels which insisted on digging up President Dwight D. Eisenhower's White House putting green?

A. The Secret Service.

Q. What former Beatle did John "Jack" Gardner Ford bring to the White House while his father was president?

A. George Harrison.

Q. Which first lady coordinated the cherry tree planting project along the Tidal Basin in Washington, D.C.?

A. Helen Taft.

Q. Where did John F. and Jacqueline Kennedy spend their honeymoon?

A. Acapulco, Mexico.

Q. Richard Nixon was a distant cousin of which two earlier twentieth-century presidents?

A. William H. Taft and Herbert Hoover.

Q. Which daughter of Richard Nixon married the grandson of Dwight D. Eisenhower, David Eisenhower II, in 1968?

A. Julie.

Q. During John F. Kennedy's presidency, what member of the presidential family received a dog named Pushinka as a gift from Soviet leader Nikita Khrushchev?

A. Caroline.

Q. Where did Jane Pierce die on December 2, 1863?

A. Andover, New Hampshire.

Q. At age three, what first lady, along with her parents, escaped in a lifeboat from the sinking HMS *Britannic*?

A. Eleanor Roosevelt.

Q. Wool produced by sheep grazing on the White House lawn during World War I was sold and provided almost $100,000 to what relief agency?

A. The Red Cross.

Q. To whom was the first telephone call made from the White House in 1878?

A. Alexander Graham Bell (called by President Rutherford B. Hayes).

Q. What was the Secret Service's code name for First Lady Nancy Reagan?

A. "Rainbow."

Q. What special receptacles did President Andrew Jackson order to be placed in the White House parlors?

A. Spittoons.

Q. To whom was the term "first lady" first applied?

A. Lucy Hayes (1877).

Q. Who was the first incumbent first lady to travel to Southeast Asia?

A. Lady Bird Johnson (1967).

Q. First Lady Lou Hoover often left what item lying on top of her bureau in her bedroom seemingly to test the honesty of the White House staff?

A. A one-thousand-dollar bill.

———◆———

Q. Who established the first White House library?

A. Abigail Fillmore.

———◆———

Q. Which first family was the first in history to walk back to the White House following the president's inauguration at the Capitol?

A. Jimmy Carter family.

———◆———

Q. Who was the first lawyer to become first lady?

A. Hillary Rodham Clinton.

———◆———

Q. What two presidential couples share January 6 as their wedding date?

A. George and Martha Washington (1759) and George and Barbara Bush (1945).

IV

PRESIDENTIAL MISCELLANEA

Q. What was the price of the coffin in which Abraham Lincoln was interred in Springfield, Illinois?

A. $75.

Q. Which president was near-sighted in one eye and far-sighted in the other?

A. James Buchanan.

Q. What four former presidents of the United States are honored on Mt. Rushmore?

A. George Washington, Thomas Jefferson, Theodore Roosevelt, and Abraham Lincoln.

Q. Which president could simultaneously write in Greek with one hand and in Latin with the other?

A. James A. Garfield.

Q. Prior to a severe heart attack in 1955, which president smoked three packs of cigarettes a day?

A. Lyndon B. Johnson.

Q. What is Ronald Reagan's middle name?

A. Wilson.

———◆———

Q. What type of revolver was used in the assassination of President William McKinley?

A. .32 Iver Johnson.

———◆———

Q. How big a settlement did Theodore Roosevelt win in a lawsuit against the editor of *Iron Age* magazine for having called Roosevelt a drunk?

A. Six cents.

———◆———

Q. Who served not only as the twenty-second but also the twenty-fourth president of the United States?

A. Grover Cleveland.

———◆———

Q. When riding in an automobile, which president generally insisted on a maximum speed of 16 miles per hour?

A. Calvin Coolidge.

———◆———

Q. Who was the first former president to die in the twentieth century?

A. Benjamin Harrison (March 13, 1901).

———◆———

Q. In what two states have mountains been named in honor of Zachary Taylor?

A. Alaska and New Mexico.

Q. Who is the only former president to serve in the U.S. Senate following his presidential term?

A. Andrew Johnson.

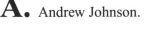

Q. Which president died heavily in debt because of his activities in the stock market?

A. Warren G. Harding.

Q. Thomas Jefferson suffered from what malady that left him nearly helpless for long periods of time?

A. Migraine headaches.

Q. Who said, "The four most miserable years of my life were my four years in the presidency"?

A. John Quincy Adams.

Q. What name was given to the 1939 Lincoln automobile customized for President Franklin D. Roosevelt's use?

A. *Sunshine Special.*

Q. What was the name of President John Adams' favorite horse?

A. Cleopatra.

Q. Who is the only former president to have an international airport named in his honor?

A. John F. Kennedy (New York City's John F. Kennedy International Airport).

Q. What 1976 movie starring Robert Redford, Dustin Hoffman, and Jason Robards revolved around the Nixon-era Watergate scandal?

A. *All the President's Men.*

Q. Who was the first chief executive to claim to be skilled in the game of billiards?

A. John Quincy Adams.

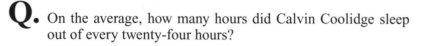

Q. In what state is the Theodore Roosevelt National Memorial Park?

A. North Dakota.

Q. What two presidents were ambidextrous?

A. Harry S. Truman and James A. Garfield.

Q. On the average, how many hours did Calvin Coolidge sleep out of every twenty-four hours?

A. Eleven.

Q. Which president owned at least eighty pairs of pants?

A. Chester Arthur.

Q. Which president expressed regret for twice having killed wild animals?

A. Ulysses S. Grant.

Q. Montana has a river named in honor of which former president?

A. Thomas Jefferson.

Q. Gamecocks were raised and fought by which chief executive?

A. Andrew Jackson.

Q. Who set a thirty-one-year longevity record as a former president?

A. Herbert Hoover.

Q. Which president only wore suits that he custom-tailored himself?

A. Andrew Johnson.

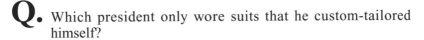

Q. Who played the role of Abraham Lincoln in the 1940 motion picture *Abe Lincoln in Illinois*?

A. Raymond Massey.

Q. Because of the tardiness of some states in ratifying the Constitution, how many states officially comprised the United States of America when George Washington was elected president?

A. Eleven (North Carolina and Rhode Island excluded).

Q. Which chief executive was superstitious about retracing his footsteps?

A. Ulysses S. Grant.

Q. On what charges were Thomas Jefferson and James Madison arrested in Vermont in the spring of 1791?

A. Carriage riding on a Sunday.

Q. Which president suffered from a nervous twitch that caused a visible and frequent jerk of his head?

A. James Buchanan.

Q. What was Herbert Hoover's middle name?

A. Clark.

Q. Although Ulysses S. Grant was very familiar with the carnage of war, what caused him to refuse to eat rare meat?

A. The sight of blood.

Q. In addition to a pair of skis, what was the only other gift accepted by Calvin Coolidge while he was president?

A. A flock of twenty-four live chickens.

Q. On the night of November 7, 1876, there was an attempt to steal the body of what former president?

A. Abraham Lincoln.

Q. What was the name of Zachary Taylor's horse, which he vowed to be "smarter than most ordinary folk and all politicians"?

A. Claybank.

Q. What was Franklin D. Roosevelt's favorite hobby?

A. Stamp collecting.

Q. Who was the first chief executive to be born a citizen of the United States of America?

A. Martin Van Buren.

Q. A Nevada mountain range is named for what nineteenth-century president?

A. Ulysses S. Grant.

Q. The Maxwell House Coffee Company's advertising slogan "It's good to the last drop" was taken from the verbal compliment of what president?

A. Theodore Roosevelt.

Q. What famous stripper claimed to have been intimate with John F. Kennedy?

A. Blaze Starr.

Q. What was the name of the private railroad car constructed in 1940 for President Franklin D. Roosevelt's use?

A. *Ferdinand Magellan.*

Q. What name did Thomas Jefferson give to his beloved mansion and estate near Charlottesville, Virginia?

A. Monticello.

Q. What was William Henry Harrison's nickname?

A. "Tippecanoe."

Q. Who was the first president to receive a pilot's license?

A. Dwight D. Eisenhower.

Q. Which president owned over three hundred slaves at the time of his death?

A. George Washington.

Q. Who was the first vice president to assume the presidency upon the death of the chief executive?

A. John Tyler.

Q. What form of salutation, which had been shunned by his presidential predecessors, did Thomas Jefferson utilize at official events?

A. Shaking hands.

Q. When did President Chester A. Arthur usually retire for the evening?

A. Not before 2:00 A.M.

Q. Who designed the likeness of Abraham Lincoln on the U.S. one-cent piece?

A. Victor D. Brenner.

Q. Early morning skinny-dipping in the Potomac River was a frequent activity of which president?

A. John Quincy Adams.

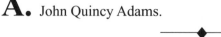

Q. What three former presidents died on July 4?

A. Thomas Jefferson and John Adams (both 1826), James Monroe (1831).

Q. Under what name did Warren G. Harding play the stock market?

A. Walter Ferguson.

Q. In whose honor was Cape Canaveral in Florida renamed from November 1963 to 1973?

A. John F. Kennedy (Cape Kennedy).

Q. To what financier did Ulysses S. Grant give most of his military swords, uniforms, medals, and battle flags as partial payment of large outstanding debts?

A. William H. Vanderbilt.

Q. In 1931 what former president earned $203,000 from writing a nationally syndicated newspaper column?

A. Calvin Coolidge.

Q. What gift did George Washington receive from the marquis de Lafayette, which Washington named Knight of Malta?

A. A Maltese jackass.

Q. At age eighty-three, what former president attempted to dispose of his home by means of a lottery to pay pressing debts?

A. Thomas Jefferson.

Q. Which president was the first to fly in an airplane?

A. Theodore Roosevelt.

Q. Who was the first chief executive to sport a full beard?

A. Abraham Lincoln.

Q. How many gun salutes were fired at one-minute intervals for the James Monroe funeral?

A. Seventy-three.

Q. The Eisenhower Center, consisting of a visitor center, library, museum, family home, and burial site, is situated in what Kansas town?

A. Abilene.

Q. Following the Civil War, who was the first president to be elected representing the Democratic Party?

A. Grover Cleveland (election of 1884).

Q. The lengthy two-volume *Memoirs* completed by Ulysses S. Grant just a few days before his death was published by what noted American literary figure?

A. Mark Twain (through Webster and Company).

Q. Which president's grave is marked by an eternal flame?

A. John F. Kennedy's.

———◆———

Q. What was the name of George Washington's long-time Virginia estate?

A. Mount Vernon.

———◆———

Q. In May 1965 while former President Dwight D. Eisenhower was visiting at Walter Reed Army Hospital, what was stolen from the trunk of his 1964 Lincoln Continental?

A. The spare tire.

———◆———

Q. Vinnie Ream became the first woman to be commissioned to create a sculpture for the United States government when she was appointed to create a life-size work of what president?

A. Abraham Lincoln.

———◆———

Q. Who was the only former president of the United States to be elected to an office in the Confederate States of America?

A. John Tyler (died before taking his seat in the Confederate House of Representatives).

———◆———

Q. Who referred to the office of president as requiring "the constitution of an athlete, the patience of a mother—and the endurance of an early Christian"?

A. Woodrow Wilson.

———◆———

Q. During whose administration did the White House make the switch from carriages to automobiles?

A. William H. Taft's (1910).

Q. Which chief executive, in reference to the presidency, said, "The buck stops here"?

A. Harry S. Truman.

Q. Bill Clinton suffers from what throat and vocal ailment?

A. Chronic laryngitis.

Q. What 1942 motion picture portrayed the political rise and political conflict of Andrew Johnson?

A. *Tennessee Johnson.*

Q. Old Whitey was the battle-proven mount of what president?

A. Zachary Taylor.

Q. Although James Monroe had wished to be buried by his wife at his Virginia estate, he was first interred at New York City, only later to be moved to what location?

A. Hollywood Cemetery, Richmond, Virginia.

Q. What noted nineteenth-century showman offered Ulysses S. Grant $100,000, plus a percentage of gate receipts, to display Grant's Civil War trophies and memorabilia?

A. Phineas T. Barnum.

Q. Although never paid for his work, what French engineer was hired by George Washington to lay out the physical plan for a new capitol for the new nation?

A. Pierre Charles L'Enfant.

Q. What president experienced recurring nightmares of being naked and lost in a foreboding primeval forest?

A. James A. Garfield.

Q. Who said that Gerald Ford was "a nice guy but he spent too much time playing football without a helmet"?

A. Lyndon B. Johnson.

Q. Which president used the words "dignified slavery" to describe his role as chief executive?

A. Andrew Jackson.

Q. Who played the role of Abraham Lincoln in director John Ford's 1939 motion picture *Young Mr. Lincoln*?

A. Henry Fonda.

Q. What personal security steps did Martin Van Buren take while presiding over the U.S. Senate during the heated debate over Andrew Jackson's withdrawal of federal deposits from the Bank of the United States?

A. He carried loaded pistols.

Q. What sum of money did Dwight D. Eisenhower receive from his book *Crusade in Europe*?

A. $650,000.

Q. How many terms as vice president did John Adams serve prior to being elected president?

A. Two.

Q. The label of what brand of vodka, introduced in Kiev in 1995, featured the likeness of President Bill Clinton wearing a traditional Ukrainian fur hat?

A. Presidential Vodka.

—◆—

Q. What former president's birthday became an official national holiday in 1892?

A. Abraham Lincoln's.

—◆—

Q. How old was John Adams when he died in 1826?

A. Ninety.

—◆—

Q. What short-lived U.S. coinage was facetiously called "the Carter Quarter"?

A. The Susan B. Anthony dollar.

—◆—

Q. Who said of Dwight D. Eisenhower, "Honor, courage, integrity, decency, all found eloquent expression in the life of this good man and noble leader"?

A. Lyndon B. Johnson.

—◆—

Q. Who was the first president to join the American Automobile Association (AAA)?

A. Woodrow Wilson.

—◆—

Q. What type of weapon was used in the assassination of President John F. Kennedy?

A. 6.5 Mannllicher Carcano Italian carbine.

Q. What famous American stuffed toy evolved from Theodore Roosevelt's refusal to shoot a bear with a cub while on a hunting trip near Yazoo City, Mississippi?

A. Teddy bear.

Q. What president's likeness first appeared on the United States dime in 1946?

A. Franklin D. Roosevelt's.

Q. During the 1800s, what three Tennessee residents served as president of the United States?

A. Andrew Jackson, James K. Polk, and Andrew Johnson.

Q. Who was known as the "Father of the Constitution"?

A. James Madison.

Q. What church did Andrew Jackson join in 1838?

A. Presbyterian.

Q. What distinction earned Theodore Roosevelt $36,735 in 1906?

A. Winning the Nobel Peace Prize.

Q. What noted philanthropist suggested that Franklin D. Roosevelt go to Warm Springs, Georgia, for rehabilitation and treatment of the crippling effects from his bout with polio?

A. George Foster Peabody.

Q. What was George Washington's religious affiliation?

A. Episcopalian.

Q. Where did the deeply indebted and somewhat forgotten James Monroe die on July 4, 1831?

A. New York City.

Q. What estate in New York was designated in 1974 as the Martin Van Buren National Historic Site?

A. Lindenwald.

Q. Theodore Roosevelt unflatteringly referred to what former president as having been "a politician of monumental little-ness"?

A. John Tyler.

Q. The John F. Kennedy Space Center is on what Florida island?

A. Merritt.

Q. What book about the federal government did Benjamin Harrison write in 1897?

A. *This Country of Ours.*

Q. Who was Dwight D. Eisenhower's Democratic opponent in both the 1952 and 1956 presidential elections?

A. Adlai E. Stevenson.

Q. With what chronic illness was Andrew Jackson afflicted during the later part of his life?

A. Tuberculosis.

Q. What president did actor Brian Keith portray in the 1975 motion picture *The Wind and the Lion*?

A. Theodore Roosevelt.

Q. James Buchanan had a pair of what large raptors at his Wheatland estate?

A. Bald eagles.

Q. Who was the first Whig candidate to be elected president of the United States?

A. William Henry Harrison.

Q. By how many electoral votes did John Adams win over Thomas Jefferson in the election of 1798?

A. Three.

Q. What president pro tempore of the Senate is considered by some political historians as having technically been the acting president of the United States for one day on March 4, 1849?

A. David R. Atchison.

Q. What was the name of Rutherford B. Hayes's estate at Fremont, Ohio?

A. Spiegel Grove.

Q. What type of revolver was used in the assassination of President James A. Garfield?

A. .44 British Bulldog.

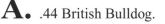

Q. Who was the second vice president to inherit the office of the president due to the death of the incumbent president?

A. Millard Fillmore.

Q. Which president is noted for being the first and only one to master the martial art of jujitsu?

A. Theodore Roosevelt.

Q. Although his request was denied by President Woodrow Wilson, which former president wanted to recruit and lead a group of special volunteers to fight in Europe during World War I?

A. Theodore Roosevelt.

Q. Who was the first chief executive to wear long trousers, rather than knee breeches, on a regular basis?

A. James Madison.

Q. The role of John F. Kennedy was played by what actor in the 1963 motion picture *PT 109*?

A. Cliff Robertson.

Q. With whom did Franklin D. Roosevelt allegedly have a long-running extramarital affair?

A. Lucy Page Mercer.

Q. John Adams's birthplace was deeded to what city in 1940?

A. Quincy, Massachusetts.

◆

Q. To what secret-rites fraternal order did Millard Fillmore belong?

A. Order of the Star-Spangled Banner.

◆

Q. Which president was given such titles as "the Little Magician" and "the Fox of Kinderhook" by his political enemies?

A. Martin Van Buren.

◆

Q. What 1995 movie dealt with an alleged love affair between Thomas Jefferson and his young slave maid, Sally Hemings?

A. *Jefferson in Paris.*

◆

Q. Who appeared on the first ten-cent stamp issued by the U.S. Post Office in 1847?

A. George Washington.

◆

Q. What was the only state that Millard Fillmore carried in the 1856 presidential election?

A. Maryland.

◆

Q. In what key did Richard Nixon state that he played every song on the piano by ear?

A. Key of G.

Q. Who wrote the books *Presidential Problems, Fishing and Shooting Sketches,* and *Good Citizenship*?

A. Grover Cleveland.

Q. What is on the reverse side of the Jefferson nickel?

A. Monticello.

Q. For which president did the U.S. Golf Association install a putting green on the grounds of the White House?

A. Dwight D. Eisenhower.

Q. What occupation did the fathers of Chester Arthur, Grover Cleveland, and Woodrow Wilson share?

A. Clergyman.

Q. As business partners on a land speculation venture, James Madison and James Monroe paid what price per acre for one thousand acres of land in the Mohawk Valley?

A. $1.50.

Q. Both Harry S. Truman and Richard Nixon played what musical instrument?

A. Piano.

Q. Weighing around 260 pounds, who was the second heaviest president?

A. Grover Cleveland (Taft was first).

Q. Because of his toughness and tenacity, what nickname was applied to Andrew Jackson?

A. "Old Hickory."

Q. In 1963 what former president had a great deal of literary success with his *Fishing for Fun—To Wash Your Soul*?

A. Herbert Hoover.

Q. James K. Polk's last name was a corruption of what old family name?

A. Pollock or Pollok.

Q. What was former President Ulysses S. Grant's last word before he died?

A. "Water."

Q. Although not noted for his great scores, who was the first president to seriously pursue the game of golf?

A. Woodrow Wilson.

Q. Who was nicknamed "Old Man Eloquent"?

A. John Quincy Adams.

Q. In a 1995 poll of 2,307 coin collectors by the Littleton Coin Company of New Hampshire, what two individuals ranked respectively in first and second place as the most popular persons to have their likenesses appear on future U.S. coins?

A. Ronald Reagan and Harry S. Truman.

Q. What noted columnist did Harry S. Truman call an SOB?

A. Drew Pearson.

Q. What color were Millard Fillmore's eyes?

A. Blue.

Q. After leaving the White House, James Buchanan wrote what book defending his policies as president?

A. *Mr. Buchanan's Administration on the Eve of the Rebellion.*

Q. Where did former President James K. Polk die on June 15, 1849?

A. Polk Place, Nashville, Tennessee.

Q. What was the name of James Buchanan's estate near Lancaster, Pennsylvania?

A. Wheatland.

Q. Millard Fillmore was a founding member and president of the Buffalo, New York, chapter of what animal rights group?

A. American Society for the Prevention of Cruelty to Animals.

Q. What former president was co-chairman of Norman Lear's People for the American Way, which opposed the influence of the Moral Majority movement?

A. Gerald Ford.

Q. Which president presented former President Harry S. Truman with a Steinway piano?

A. Richard Nixon.

Q. How tall was Benjamin Harrison?

A. Five feet, six inches.

Q. What piece of equipment did President Calvin Coolidge utilize to supplant his love of horseback riding during his term at the White House?

A. An electric mechanical horse.

Q. What former president is buried at Woodward Hill Cemetery, Lancaster, Pennsylvania?

A. James Buchanan.

Q. Though Zachary Taylor neither drank liquor nor smoked tobacco, he did enjoy what source of nicotine?

A. Chewing tobacco.

Q. Whose portrait appears on the official seal and flag of the State of Washington?

A. George Washington's.

Q. What is George Bush's full name?

A. George Herbert Walker Bush.

Q. What ailment brought about the death of former President Andrew Johnson on July 31, 1875?

A. Stroke.

Q. On February 6, 1968, what former president fulfilled a golfer's dream at Palm Springs, California, by getting a hole in one?

A. Dwight D. Eisenhower.

Q. For what record number of days did Franklin D. Roosevelt serve as president of the United States?

A. 4,422.

Q. The Lincoln Memorial has been used as a design motif on what two denominations of United States money?

A. The one-cent piece and the five-dollar bill.

Q. Millard Fillmore declined an honorary degree from what university, stating that he had not earned such an honor?

A. Oxford.

Q. Upon receiving a cable message from portly William H. Taft stating that he had been on a twenty-five-mile horseback ride, Secretary of War Elihu Root cabled back what question to the president?

A. "How is the horse?"

Q. How much did James Madison weigh?

A. About one hundred pounds.

Q. Who has been the only president to be honored by having his likeness placed on a U.S. coin while living?

A. Calvin Coolidge (the 1926 sesquicentennial half-dollar).

◆

Q. Of whom did Henry "Lighthorse Harry" Lee make the statement, "First in war, first in peace, and first in the hearts of his countrymen"?

A. George Washington.

◆

Q. Which two presidents were signers of the Declaration of Independence?

A. Thomas Jefferson and John Adams.

◆

Q. Robert Mills designed what presidential memorial?

A. Washington Monument.

◆

Q. "Ask not what your country can do for you, but ask what you can do for your country," were the words of what president?

A. John F. Kennedy.

◆

Q. Ulysses S. Grant, who succumbed to throat cancer, smoked how many cigars a day?

A. Twenty.

◆

Q. In 1971 which former president was honored when his likeness was placed on a dollar coin?

A. Dwight D. Eisenhower.

Q. Which former president's personal library of more than six thousand books became the nucleus for the Library of Congress?

A. Thomas Jefferson's.

Q. Who became president of the United States without having been elected as president or vice president?

A. Gerald Ford.

Q. Which two presidents signed the Constitution?

A. George Washington and James Madison.

Q. What foreign capital is named in honor of a U.S. president?

A. Monrovia, Liberia (for James Monroe).

Q. Although many of his contemporaries believed tomatoes to be poisonous, who was the first president to cultivate and eat this fruit?

A. Thomas Jefferson.

Q. Abraham Lincoln, Andrew Johnson, Ulysses S. Grant, and James A. Garfield all died having neglected to do what?

A. Leave a will.

Q. What was Warren G. Harding's middle name?

A. Gamaliel.

Q. In 1826 James Madison became rector (president) of what institution of higher learning?

A. University of Virginia.

———◆———

Q. Adopted in 1938, the official flag of Washington, D.C., is based on the color scheme and design of whose family coat of arms?

A. George Washington's.

———◆———

Q. What former president stated that "Richard Nixon is a no-good lying bastard"?

A. Harry S. Truman.

———◆———

Q. Director Oliver Stone wove together a controversial tale of conspiracy in what 1991 motion picture about President John F. Kennedy's assassination?

A. *JFK.*

———◆———

Q. In addition to Shakespearean productions, what American play did William McKinley especially enjoy?

A. *Rip Van Winkle.*

———◆———

Q. On October 14, 1912, while Theodore Roosevelt was campaigning for the presidency on the Progressive Party ticket, who attempted to assassinate him in Milwaukee, Wisconsin?

A. John Flammang Schrank.

———◆———

Q. What did Calvin Coolidge use to slick down his hair?

A. Petroleum jelly.

Q. Who was the only president to receive a patent which consisted of a proposed means to help lift boats over shoals?

A. Abraham Lincoln (May 29, 1847).

———◆———

Q. How many state capitals are named for U.S. presidents?

A. Four (Jackson, Mississippi; Jefferson City, Missouri; Lincoln, Nebraska; and Madison, Wisconsin).

———◆———

Q. What was Ulysses S. Grant's actual name?

A. Hiram Ulysses Grant.

———◆———

Q. A special cottage on the grounds of what famous golf course bears the name of Dwight D. Eisenhower, who often played there?

A. Augusta National (Georgia).

———◆———

Q. Which chief executive requested that upon his death his body be wrapped in a U.S. flag and his head rested on a copy of the Constitution of the United States?

A. Andrew Johnson.

———◆———

Q. What woodwind instrument does Bill Clinton play?

A. Saxophone.

———◆———

Q. Though various theories of conspiracy have been presented, who did the Warren Commission conclude to have acted alone in the assassination of President John F. Kennedy?

A. Lee Harvey Oswald.

Q. Where is the Jimmy Carter Library and the Carter Center?

A. Atlanta, Georgia.

Q. The eighteenth, nineteenth, and twentieth presidents all were born in which state?

A. Ohio (Grant, Hayes, and Garfield).

Q. Because of his adherence to the Confederacy, what former president's death was purposely ignored by the Federal government?

A. John Tyler's.

Q. Of which president did humorist Will Rogers say, "He didn't do nothing, but that's what we wanted done"?

A. Calvin Coolidge.

Q. Upon receiving notice of George Washington's death, Napoleon Bonaparte declared how many days of mourning in France?

A. Ten.

Q. Who created the sculpture of Abraham Lincoln that graces the Lincoln Memorial in Washington, D.C.?

A. Daniel Chester French.

Q. Where is the Gerald R. Ford Museum?

A. Ann Arbor, Michigan.

Q. The Lyndon B. Johnson Library and Museum is in which Texas city?

A. Austin.

Q. Who was the first vice president of the United States?

A. John Adams.

Q. Which former president is buried at Plymouth Notch Cemetery in Plymouth Notch, Vermont?

A. Calvin Coolidge.

Q. In 1646 which president's great-great-great-grandfather Cornelius Maessen purchased a plantation which basically was the site of present-day Greenwich Village, New York?

A. Martin Van Buren.

Q. What does the "S" in Harry S. Truman's name stand for?

A. It stands for nothing.

Q. *Scribner's Magazine* paid which president $50,000 for his personal account of his big-game hunting experiences in Africa?

A. Theodore Roosevelt.

Q. What Federalist candidate and former minister to France lost to James Madison in the election of 1808?

A. C. C. Pinckney.

Q. In what year did John F. Kennedy's likeness first appear on a half-dollar coin?

A. 1964.

Q. With reference to his golf game, which president said he was known as "the jinx of the links"?

A. Gerald Ford.

Q. Measuring 55 feet, 1⅛ inches along the base of each of its four sides, what is the height of the great obelisk of the Washington Monument?

A. 555 feet, 5⅛ inches.

Q. Which former president's last words were, "I have tried so hard to do right"?

A. Grover Cleveland.

Q. Who was the first president to utilize makeup for his television appearances?

A. Dwight D. Eisenhower.

Q. Throughout his life, what president had numerous nightmares with the recurring theme of paralysis?

A. Lyndon B. Johnson.

Q. What noted American writer died in 1864 while vacationing with former President Franklin Pierce in the White Mountains in New Hampshire?

A. Nathaniel Hawthorne.

Q. Millard Fillmore is buried in what Buffalo, New York, cemetery?

A. Forest Lawn.

Q. Thomas Jefferson's self-penned epitaph excluded mentioning what public office he had held?

A. President of the United States.

Q. What was the name of Andrew Jackson's racehorse that during its prime was never beaten in the two-mile race?

A. Truxton.

Q. What was the caliber of the single-shot derringer used in the assassination of President Abraham Lincoln?

A. .44 caliber.

Q. Who said, "I'm a conservative, but I'm not a nut about it"?

A. George Bush.

Q. How long did James K. Polk live following his retirement from the presidency?

A. Three months.

Q. Who conducted the graveside service of former President Lyndon B. Johnson in 1973?

A. The Reverend Billy Graham.

Q. Reflecting on the assassination of President Abraham Lincoln, who said, "Next to the destruction of the Confederacy, the death of Abraham Lincoln was the darkest day the South has ever known"?

A. Jefferson Davis.

———◆———

Q. What color were George Washington's eyes?

A. Blue gray.

———◆———

Q. Who not only held the highest position in the executive branch of the government, but also the highest position in the judicial branch of the government?

A. William H. Taft (president of the United States and chief justice of the Supreme Court).

———◆———

Q. While on a hunting trip in Maine, Benjamin Harrison shot what type of animal, mistakenly thinking it to be a raccoon?

A. A pig.

———◆———

Q. What was Chester Arthur's middle name?

A. Alan.

———◆———

Q. Prior to World War I, Dwight D. Eisenhower's brother Arthur roomed at a Kansas City boarding house with what future president?

A. Harry S. Truman.

———◆———

Q. What is Jimmy Carter's full name?

A. James Earl Carter, Jr.

Q. What legislative body selected Martin Van Buren's running mate, Richard M. Johnson, as vice president in February 1837?

A. The U.S. Senate.

Q. In which two years did three different individuals serve as president of the United States?

A. 1841 (Martin Van Buren, William Henry Harrison, John Tyler) and 1881 (Rutherford B. Hayes, James A. Garfield, Chester A. Arthur).

Q. What was Calvin Coolidge's first name?

A. John.

Q. In 1954, former President Harry S. Truman had to undergo emergency surgery for what ailment?

A. Gallbladder attack.

Q. What close associate of Andrew Jackson was sometimes referred to as "Young Hickory"?

A. James K. Polk.

Q. What first talking movie for director D. W. Griffith, starring Walter Huston and based on the life of a popular U.S. president, was Griffith's last motion picture?

A. *Abraham Lincoln* (1930).

Q. How tall was George Washington as an adult?

A. Six feet, two inches.

Q. In 1947 what dam on the Colorado River was officially renamed Hoover Dam by Congress to honor former President Herbert Hoover?

A. Boulder Dam.

Q. Which president had a horse named Jeff Davis?

A. Ulysses S. Grant.

Q. Commenting on his religious creed, what president said, "My belief embraces the Divinity of Christ and a recognition of Christianity as the mightiest factor in the world's civilization"?

A. William McKinley.

Q. What was John Adams's political affiliation?

A. Federalist.

Q. What three coins did Dwight D. Eisenhower carry in his pocket for luck?

A. A five-guinea gold piece, a franc, and a silver dollar.

Q. Who was elected two times as vice president and also twice as president?

A. Richard Nixon.

Q. During his trial on charges of assassinating James A. Garfield, who did Charles J. Guiteau say instructed him to kill the president?

A. God.

Q. In 1976 what highest military title was bestowed by the U.S. Congress on George Washington?

A. General of the Armies of the United States.

Q. What colorful frontiersman and legislator made the unflattering comparison "as dung is to a diamond" of Martin Van Buren to Andrew Jackson?

A. Davy Crockett.

Q. Because of his religious commitment, what subject did William Henry Harrison refuse to discuss on Sunday?

A. Politics.

Q. Why did Richard Nixon comb his hair straight back?

A. To cover a scar.

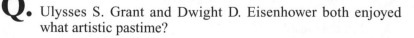

Q. What candidate did the aged former President Herbert Hoover endorse in the 1964 presidential election?

A. Barry Goldwater.

Q. Chester Arthur was afflicted with what kidney ailment?

A. Bright's disease.

Q. Ulysses S. Grant and Dwight D. Eisenhower both enjoyed what artistic pastime?

A. Painting.

Q. Which former president requested that no bells be rung at his funeral?

A. Martin Van Buren.

Q. Speed-reader Jimmy Carter was clocked at how many words per minute, while maintaining a 95 percent comprehension level?

A. 2,000 words per minute.

Q. Who was the first chief executive to play tennis?

A. Theodore Roosevelt.

Q. Who unsuccessfully ran on the Democratic Party's ticket against Ulysses S. Grant in the election of 1868?

A. Horatio Seymour.

Q. While in the White House, how did President Herbert Hoover exercise each morning before breakfast?

A. By tossing a medicine ball.

Q. Martin Van Buren's coffin was constructed of what material?

A. Rosewood.

Q. Although it is popularly known as "Grant's Tomb," what is the formal name of America's largest mausoleum?

A. General Grant National Memorial.

Q. Which president did Andrew Jackson refer to as "the imbecile chief"?

A. William Henry Harrison.

Q. What type of flag draped the casket of former President John Tyler?

A. Confederate States of America.

Q. What mid-nineteenth-century president's personal library consisted of some 4,000 volumes?

A. Millard Fillmore.

Q. Dwight D. Eisenhower and his five brothers were all called by what nickname at some time in their lives?

A. "Ike."

Q. Which president was buried at a site he had personally marked by planting a shoot taken from a willow tree at the site of Napoleon's original tomb on Saint Helena?

A. Andrew Johnson.

Q. How tall was Abraham Lincoln?

A. Six feet, four inches.

Q. Who spoke of President John Tyler as being one "with talents not above mediocrity"?

A. John Quincy Adams.

Q. Which president stated that he was often frequented in his dreams by the memories of an actress he had known in Paris in his youth?

A. John Quincy Adams.

Q. What governor of the Utah Territory stated, "Zachary Taylor is dead and gone to hell, and I am glad of it!"?

A. Brigham Young.

Q. How much did William H. Taft weigh?

A. 300 to 340 pounds.

Q. Who was the first Roman Catholic to be elected president of the United States?

A. John F. Kennedy.

Q. While visiting in France, former President Millard Fillmore bailed what noted American newspaper publisher out of the Paris jail?

A. Horace Greeley.

Q. After leaving the White House, Franklin and Jane Pierce lived on what Atlantic island for two years?

A. Madeira.

Q. Where did the Ronald Reagan Presidential Library open in November 1991?

A. Simi Valley, California.

Q. What animal that wandered onto the White House grounds and was adopted by President Herbert Hoover later became the mascot of a boys' ball team in Hyattsville, Maryland?

A. An opossum.

Q. Who did Theodore Roosevelt say "was the best man I ever knew"?

A. His father (Theodore Roosevelt, Sr.).

Q. How many years did John Quincy Adams serve in the House of Representives following his term as president?

A. Seventeen.

Q. The severe bouts of chronic depression that plagued Franklin Pierce were in part caused by his battle with what self-induced malady?

A. Alcoholism.

Q. Which golfing president regularly shot in the upper seventies?

A. John F. Kennedy.

Q. Following his assassination, Abraham Lincoln's body lay in state in how many cities?

A. Fourteen.

Q. How tall was Ulysses S. Grant?

A. Five feet, seven inches.

Q. What was Herbert Hoover's religious background?

A. Quaker.

———◆———

Q. What musical instrument did both Thomas Jefferson and John Tyler play?

A. Violin.

———◆———

Q. Former President Chester Arthur served as president of what railroad?

A. New York Arcade Railway Company.

———◆———

Q. What name did Grover Cleveland give to his favorite hunting rifle?

A. "Death and Destruction."

———◆———

Q. Who penned *This Country of Ours* and *Views of an Ex-President*?

A. Benjamin Harrison.

———◆———

Q. How much shorter was John F. Kennedy's left leg than his right leg?

A. Three-quarters of an inch.

———◆———

Q. Although several chief executives have been avid fishermen, which president was a member of the exclusive Restigouche Salmon Club?

A. Chester A. Arthur.

Q. Throughout his life William McKinley was a devout and active member of what religious denomination?

A. Methodist.

Q. Which former president died at the Exchange Hotel in Richmond, Virginia, on January 18, 1862?

A. John Tyler.

Q. What type of literature did Herbert Hoover enjoy reading?

A. Mysteries.

———————◆———————

Q. Who was the first president to be popularly known in the press by his initials?

A. Theodore Roosevelt (TR).

———————◆———————

Q. What was Dwight D. Eisenhower's actual name?

A. David Dwight Eisenhower.

———————◆———————

Q. What apparatus did former President Grover Cleveland use on himself to relieve severe bouts of indigestion?

A. A stomach pump.

Q. Other than George Washington, who was the only president to regularly participate in the equestrian sport of riding to the hounds?

A. Theodore Roosevelt.

Q. In which Washington, D.C., church was President John F. Kennedy's funeral mass held?

A. St. Matthew's Cathedral.

Q. How many times was Franklin D. Roosevelt elected or re-elected to the office of president of the United States?

A. Four.

Q. Visitors often plucked what souvenirs from Zachary Taylor's horse, Old Whitey, which grazed on the White House lawn?

A. Hairs from his tail.

Q. In writing to his daughter Martha, Thomas Jefferson referred to what creature as "a superior being in the form of a bird"?

A. The mockingbird.

Q. Who played the role of Richard Nixon in Oliver Stone's motion picture *Nixon*?

A. Anthony Hopkins.

Q. In 1991 which former president's body was exhumed to test for what proved to be erroneous reports of arsenic poisoning?

A. Zachary Taylor.

Q. As chief justice, who dedicated the Lincoln Memorial in Washington, D.C., in May 1922?

A. William H. Taft.

Q. Former President George Bush dropped his lifetime membership in what organization in May 1995?

A. NRA (National Rifle Association).

Q. Woodrow Wilson was an avid player of what card game?

A. Bridge.

Q. How many presidential successors were present at former President Richard Nixon's funeral in 1994?

A. Five (Ford, Carter, Reagan, Bush, and Clinton).

Q. In what year did George Washington's likeness first appear on the U.S. quarter?

A. 1932.

Q. A collection of poems by what former president was published under the title of *Always a Reckoning* in 1994?

A. Jimmy Carter.

Q. Which former president is buried in Concord, New Hampshire?

A. Franklin Pierce.

Q. Which president soaked his feet in cold water each morning, believing the practice would keep him from catching colds?

A. Thomas Jefferson.

Q. What was Andrew Jackson's favorite main dish?

A. Turkey hash.

Q. The state of Alaska has a mountain and an ice field named in honor of which former president?

A. William McKinley.

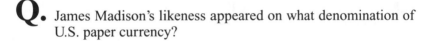

Q. In what state is Lyndon B. Johnson's birthday recognized as a legal holiday?

A. Texas.

Q. James Madison's likeness appeared on what denomination of U.S. paper currency?

A. Five-thousand-dollar bill.

———◆———

Q. Which tone-deaf president remarked, "I only know two tunes, one of them is 'Yankee Doodle' and the other isn't"?

A. Ulysses S. Grant.

———◆———

Q. Theodore Roosevelt Island, an 88-acre natural area, is situated in the middle of what river?

A. Potomac River.

———◆———

Q. Following the assassination of President Abraham Lincoln, who was the next incumbent president to visit Ford's Theater in Washington, D.C.?

A. Gerald Ford.

Q. What is Gerald Ford's middle name?

A. Rudolph.

Q. What new name did Congress assign the National Cultural Center in Washington, D.C., to honor a former president?

A. John F. Kennedy Center for the Performing Arts.

Q. Who is credited with inventing the swivel chair?

A. Thomas Jefferson.

Q. Where was President Richard Nixon's California White House?

A. San Clemente.

Q. Nathaniel Hawthorne's last book, *Our Old Home,* was dedicated to what former president and lifelong friend?

A. Franklin Pierce.

Q. Since the beginning of the publication of *Time* magazine in 1923, who holds the record for most appearances on the magazine's cover?

A. Richard Nixon (56 times as of December 1995).

Q. How many pounds did Theodore Roosevelt lose during a 1913 expedition in Brazil?

A. Fifty-seven pounds.

Q. Although a box office flop, what 1944 presidential motion picture directed by Henry King won five Oscars?

A. *Wilson.*

———◆———

Q. Who is the earliest president of whom a photograph exists?

A. John Quincy Adams (taken after his presidency).

———◆———

Q. In what year did the Lincoln Memorial first appear on the reverse side of the U.S. one-cent piece?

A. 1959.

The Presidents of the United States

President	Born	Birthplace	Political party	Age at inauguration
1. George Washington	Feb. 22, 1732	Westmoreland County, Va.	None	57
2. John Adams	Oct. 30, 1735	Braintree, Mass.	Federalist	61
3. Thomas Jefferson	Apr. 13, 1743	Albemarle County, Va.	Democratic-Republican	57
4. James Madison	Mar. 16, 1751	Port Conway, Va.	Democratic-Republican	57
5. James Monroe	Apr. 28, 1758	Westmoreland County, Va.	Democratic-Republican	58
6. John Quincy Adams	July 11, 1767	Braintree, Mass.	Democratic-Republican	57
7. Andrew Jackson	Mar. 15, 1767	Waxhaw Settlement, S.C.	Democratic	61
8. Martin Van Buren	Dec. 5, 1782	Kinderhook, N.Y.	Democratic	54
9. William H. Harrison	Feb. 9, 1773	Berkeley, Va.	Whig	68
10. John Tyler	Mar. 29, 1790	Greenway, Va.	Whig	51
11. James K. Polk	Nov. 2, 1795	near Pineville, N.C.	Democratic	49
12. Zachary Taylor	Nov. 24, 1784	Orange County, Va.	Whig	64
13. Millard Fillmore	Jan. 7, 1800	Locke, N.Y.	Whig	50
14. Franklin Pierce	Nov. 23, 1804	Hillsboro, N.H.	Democratic	48
15. James Buchanan	Apr. 23, 1791	near Mercersburg, Pa.	Democratic	65
16. Abraham Lincoln	Feb. 12, 1809	near Hodgenville, Ky.	Republican, Union[†]	52
17. Andrew Johnson	Dec. 29, 1808	Raleigh, N.C.	Union[‡]	56
18. Ulysses S. Grant	Apr. 27, 1822	Point Pleasant, Ohio	Republican	46
19. Rutherford B. Hayes	Oct. 4, 1822	Delaware, Ohio	Republican	54
20. James A. Garfield	Nov. 19, 1831	Orange, Ohio	Republican	49
21. Chester A. Arthur	Oct. 5, 1829	Fairfield, Vt.	Republican	51
22. Grover Cleveland	Mar. 18, 1837	Caldwell, N.J.	Democratic	47
23. Benjamin Harrison	Aug. 20, 1833	North Bend, Ohio	Republican	55
24. Grover Cleveland	Mar. 18, 1837	Caldwell, N.J.	Democratic	55
25. William McKinley	Jan. 29, 1843	Niles, Ohio	Republican	54
26. Theodore Roosevelt	Oct. 27, 1858	New York, N.Y.	Republican	42
27. William H. Taft	Sept. 15, 1857	Cincinnati, Ohio	Republican	51
28. Woodrow Wilson	Dec. 29, 1856	Staunton, Va.	Democratic	56
29. Warren G. Harding	Nov. 2, 1865	near Blooming Grove, Ohio	Republican	55
30. Calvin Coolidge	July 4, 1872	Plymouth Notch, Vt.	Republican	51
31. Herbert C. Hoover	Aug. 10, 1874	West Branch, Iowa	Republican	54
32. Franklin D. Roosevelt	Jan. 30, 1882	Hyde Park, N.Y.	Democratic	51
33. Harry S Truman	May 8, 1884	Lamar, Mo.	Democratic	60
34. Dwight D. Eisenhower	Oct. 14, 1890	Denison, Tex.	Republican	62
35. John F. Kennedy	May 29, 1917	Brookline, Mass.	Democratic	43
36. Lyndon B. Johnson	Aug. 27, 1908	near Stonewall, Tex.	Democratic	55

†The Union Party was made up of Republicans and War Democrats
‡The Union Party was made up of Republicans and War Democrats; Johnson was a War Democrat

Served	Died	College or University	Religion	Vice President
1789-1797	Dec. 14, 1799		Episcopalian	John Adams
1797-1801	July 4, 1826	Harvard	Unitarian	Thomas Jefferson
1801-1809	July 4, 1826	William and Mary	Unitarian	Aaron Burr
				George Clinton
1809-1817	June 28, 1836	Princeton	Episcopalian	George Clinton
				Elbridge Gerry
1817-1825	July 4, 1831	William and Mary	Episcopalian	Daniel Tompkins
1825-1829	Feb. 23, 1848	Harvard	Unitarian	John C. Calhoun
1829-1837	June 8, 1845		Presbyterian	John C. Calhoun
				Martin Van Buren
1837-1841	July 24, 1862		Dutch Reformed	Richard Johnson
1841	Apr. 4, 1841	Hampden-Sydney	Episcopalian	John Tyler
1841-1845	Jan. 18, 1862	William and Mary	Episcopalian	
1845-1849	June 15, 1849	Univ. N. Carolina	Methodist	George M. Dallas
1849-1850	July 9, 1850		Episcopalian	Millard Fillmore
1850-1853	Mar. 8, 1874		Unitarian	
1853-1857	Oct. 8, 1869	Bowdoin	Episcopalian	William R. King
1857-1861	June 1, 1868	Dickinson	Presbyterian	John Breckinridge
1861-1865	Apr. 15, 1865		Presbyterian	Hannibal Hamblin
				Andrew Johnson
1865-1869	July 31, 1875	Methodist		
1869-1877	July 23, 1885	U.S. Mil. Academy	Methodist	Schuyler Colfax
				Henry Wilson
1877-1881	Jan. 17, 1893	Kenyon	Methodist	William A. Wheeler
1881	Sept. 19, 1881	Williams	Disciples of Christ	Chester A. Arthur
1881-1885	Nov. 18, 1886	Union	Episcopalian	
1885-1889	June 24, 1908		Presbyterian	Thomas A. Hendricks
1889-1893	Mar. 13, 1901	Miami	Presbyterian	Levi P. Morton
1893-1897	June 24, 1908		Presbyterian	Adlai E. Stevenson
1897-1901	Sept. 14, 1901	Allegheny College	Methodist	Garret A. Hobart
				Theodore Roosevelt
1901-1909	Jan. 6, 1919	Harvard	Dutch Reformed	Charles W. Fairbanks
1909-1913	Mar. 8, 1930	Yale	Unitarian	James S. Sherman
1913-1921	Feb. 3, 1924	Princeton	Presbyterian	Thomas R. Marshall
1921-1923	Aug. 2, 1923		Baptist	Calvin Coolidge
1923-1929	Jan. 5, 1933	Amherst	Congregationist	Charles G. Dawes
1929-1933	Oct. 20, 1964	Stanford	Friend (Quaker)	Charles Curtis
1933-1945	Apr. 12, 1945	Harvard	Episcopalian	John N. Garner
				Henry A. Wallace
				Harry S Truman
1945-1953	Dec. 26, 1972		Baptist	Alben W. Barkley
1953-1961	Mar. 28, 1969	U.S. Mil. Academy	Presbyterian	Richard M. Nixon
1961-1963	Nov. 22, 1963	Harvard	Roman Catholic	Lyndon B. Johnson
1963-1969	Jan. 22, 1973	SW Texas State	Disciples of Christ	Hubert H. Humphrey

PRESIDENTIAL TRIVIA

President	Born	Birthplace	Political party	Age at inauguration
37. Richard M. Nixon	Jan. 9, 1913	Yorba Linda, Calif.	Republican	56
38. Gerald R. Ford*	July 14, 1913	Omaha, Neb.	Republican	61
39. Jimmy Carter	Oct. 1, 1924	Plains, Ga.	Democratic	52
40. Ronald W. Reagan	Feb. 6, 1911	Tampico, Ill.	Republican	69
41. George H. W. Bush	June 12, 1924	Milton, Mass.	Republican	64
42. Bill Clinton	Aug. 19, 1946	Hope, Ark.	Democratic	46

* Inaugurated Aug. 9, 1974, to replace Nixon, who resigned on the same day

Served	Died	College or University	Religion	Vice President
1969-1974	Apr. 22, 1994	Whittier	Friend (Quaker)	Spiro T. Agnew Gerald R. Ford¶
1974-1977		Michigan	Episcopalian	Nelson Rockefeller§
1977-1981		U.S. Naval Academy	Baptist	Walter F. Mondale
1981-1989		Eureka	Disciples of Christ	George H. W. Bush
1989-1993		Yale	Episcopalian	Dan Quayle
1993-		Georgetown	Baptist	Al Gore

¶Inaugurated Dec. 6, 1973, to replace Agnew, who reigned Oct. 10, 1973.
§Inaugurated Dec. 19, 1974, to replace Ford, who became president Aug. 9, 1974.

Ernie Couch is the owner of Consultx, a support
firm for the publishing industry specializing in
advertising and graphic design. He has written
nearly twenty trivia books, many with his wife, Jill.
They live in Antioch, Tennessee.